THE
SATURDAY MORNING
SONG
CHRONICLES

Memoirs, Motown, and Music

by
Paul B Allen III

Cover Design: Paul B Allen III
Cover Photography: Alice Pasqual

Publisher: Paul B Allen III City of Henderson, Nevada, USA
https://pba3.com/contact

Editor: Paul B Allen III City of Henderson, Nevada, USA

Library of Congress Control Number: 2020915241

ISBN 978-1-7355721-0-9
1. Memoirs 2. Biographies 3. Music Business 4. Music Reference

First Edition Printed in Henderson, Nevada, USA

Contents

Preface

The Saturday Morning Song Chronicles was a column that consisted of a series of 52 articles written between 2019 and 2020. Each Saturday morning, excited family, friends, and fans would arise, looking forward to discovering the hidden gems presented in *The Chronicles* for that weekend.

I worked hard to bring my readers new and fascinating information from the world of music; however, *The Chronicles* dealt with music from the past, presenting little known facts about the songs and artists they knew and loved. It also introduced them to artists who were significant, but whose names and contributions are now little more than footnotes in time.

Some described reading *The Saturday Morning Song Chronicles* as being like "getting into a time machine" that took them back to the days of their youth. They loved the feeling of nostalgia the articles evoked. Many hated when the experience was over, and they had to come back to our present, uneasy times. Then, they would begin the week-long wait until they could be taken back in time once more.

Others mentioned how much they enjoyed the personal stories I added. As a professional singer (lead vocalist of the Platters), and a number one hit songwriter, I have worked with several of the artists I featured in *The Chronicles*. So, I shared stories and insights with my readers that no one else had ever heard before.

As the column evolved, readership became international. I was amazed.

To emphasize or demonstrate the points of each article, I researched videos and provided the links to them on YouTube, which added significantly to the overall experience.

When the final installment of *The Saturday Morning Song Chronicles* published, I received hundreds of comments lamenting that something so thoroughly enjoyed was being taken away. I was overwhelmed by the powerful and emotional reactions.

I also learned that many more people had been reading *The Chronicles* than I realized. They had never made comments before, but they had been reading all along. Now they were writing and sharing with me how *The Saturday Morning Song Chronicles* impacted their lives. Those comments touched my heart, and they also made me sad that I had brought *The Chronicles* to an end.

A book, gathering those articles together, seemed to now make perfect sense. *The Chronicles* were not dead, they were evolving, and most found solace in that fact.

At the end of each chapter, look for the Referenced Videos section. There you will find links to all videos mentioned in each chapter. Viewing the videos after reading the stories creates an enchanting experience and will help you see the music you have known for years in a completely new light.

A caveat. YouTube periodically changes the links to some videos. If this happens, you now have the name of the song and the artist. Type these into the YouTube search box and you will generally find the video that was referenced in the article.

For those who love the tactile feel of books and choose to purchase the printed version of *The Saturday Morning Song Chronicles*, the listed links will not be clickable for you. But here is a dedicated page with every listed link made clickable because life should be easy.

You can type in this URL https://bit.ly/2Ywajl3, or scan this QR Code and then click on the VIDEO LINK PAGE FOR THE SATURDAY MORNING SONG CHRONICLES. Enjoy!

Chapter 1 – Nancy Wilson

It was 1976. I was 23 years old, and if I remember correctly, it was a Monday afternoon.

I smiled as I walked toward The Record Plant, a recording studio in Hollywood. I had just made a discovery, and I could not have been more pleased with myself.

I heard a car pull up. I turned to watch as it stopped at the parking meter.

She got out. She was even more beautiful than her album covers would lead one to believe. She was thirty-nine years old and drop-dead gorgeous. She opened her purse, reaching for change as she stood next to the parking meter. Boldly, I decided to share my discovery with her.

"Put in a dime. It will get you the same time as a quarter will." She looked at me. You know, the look that says, "I have no idea who you are or why you are talking to me or why I should believe you." But she nodded to me, put in a dime, and got the same time on the meter as if she had dropped in a quarter. She turned to me and laughed. "You just saved me fifteen cents."

I waited for her, and we headed toward the studio entrance together. I extended my hand. "Hi, I'm Paul Allen." She smiled warmly and shook my hand. "Nancy Wilson." I held the door of the studio recording room open for Ms. Wilson so that she could enter first. I got another sweet smile as she walked past me.

But her producer, Gene McDaniels, was not smiling. Not at me, anyway. He looked bothered by the fact that I was walking in with Nancy. His vibe was strange, and the tension was palpable, at least it was to me.

Didn't he invite me to come today? I asked myself silently. *Did I misunderstand? When he visited my father's house this weekend, he said he was producing Nancy Wilson, and that we could come and watch.*

Ah, we could come and watch. But there was no we. Only I had come. My father, whom Gene knew well (my grandfather and father had helped Gene get into the music business decades earlier), was unable to make the trip. I, whom Gene barely knew at all, was there, smiling, already buddies with the star he was producing. I was just some kid, crashing his party, who had found favor with this fabulous artist, and Gene did not take kindly to that notion.

Gene warmly greeted Nancy as she settled in next to him behind the large mixing board. He barely said two words to me. But if looks could kill?

I sat on the sofa located just in front of that board, whereas the mixing board itself sat on a platform or riser. I figured I had better be as quiet and as invisible as possible. I was embarrassed, but I could not retreat.

There was an artist in the recording portion of the studio, just behind the sizeable soundproof window we all observed him through. He was playing one of those new keyboards called a synthesizer. The purpose was to give Nancy a modern jazzy sound to the track she was about to perform.

As we could all hear through the studio monitors as he played, this musician was remarkable. He finished, exited the soundproofed room, then stood next to me as I sat on the couch. We looked at each other, smiled and nodded in recognition.

I wanted to tell him so badly that I thought he had mad skills and that he just killed that synth part on the track, but I was sure as heck not going to say anything to him, for fear it would put Gene into labor.

(It was not until later that day when I stopped at Tower Records on Sunset Boulevard before heading back home to San Bernardino that I had a revelation. There was a section in the store featuring one artist, his latest album being displayed maybe eight across in four rows, with the artist's face smiling from the album cover. The name of the album was *Liberated Fantasies*.

Man, this guy looks familiar, I thought. Then it hit me. It was the face I had just seen in the studio! That keyboard player who looked down at me, smiled, and nodded as I sat on the sofa was George Duke, and I had just witnessed him performing musical magic on the Nancy Wilson album called *This Mother's Daughter*.)

Next, Nancy was up, but before she went through the door into the actual recording area, Gene said, "Listen, I will be glad to clear the studio while you do your vocals." I felt the dagger in my heart. *Jesus, this guy wants to get rid of me. Maybe I should go*, I thought.

But in that very moment, Nancy Wilson made me fall head over heels in love with her.

She could see what was happening. She looked at me for a moment; then, she turned to Gene and said, "I'm a pro. I perform in front of people every day. Having someone in the studio while I record is no big deal at all."

"Are you sure?" Gene continued, "Because I have no problem clearing the studio."

Man—is he ever pushing the issue!

Nancy just smiled and said again, "No need. Everything's fine."

After returning to San Bernardino later that night, my father asked me how things went on my visit to the studio.

I told him everything was fantastic.

The moral of this story?

It is incredible what a person will do for you if you save them fifteen cents.

I love you, Nancy Wilson. You were a class act, even when the rest of the world was not watching.

***

Referenced Videos:

"A Lot of Living to Do"
https://bit.ly/3cpuWmF

"The Sweetest Sounds"
https://bit.ly/2MnFCrf

Chapter 2 – Otis Redding

Lefty Gomez of the 1930s New York Yankees baseball team was one of the greatest pitchers of all time, but, according to *The Society for American Baseball Research*, "Once after an inning in which three hard-hit balls were run down and caught by his outfielders, he [Lefty Gomez] said, 'I'd rather be lucky than good.'"

Back before the days of digital music, before there were mobile phones or MP3 players (or MP3 files), before Spotify or Pandora or pcs or Apples (except for Red Delicious, of which I was particularly fond), there were very few ways to hear or discover new music.

There were television programs, like *The Ed Sullivan Show*. There were mom and pop record shops (like A&A Records in Omaha, Nebraska, owned and operated by my grandparents), where the sales attendant (me, for the summer of 1971) would make recommendations based on the new music received from distributors that the general public had not yet heard.

However, the way most of us heard new music back then was by listening to the brick and mortar radio stations that dotted the landscape of our nation.

At that time, just like now, people loved their TVs. But by and large, they listened to their music on radios, and the radio stations were providing great new music every day, free of charge. No monthly subscription required.

All you had to do was turn on your radio, tune in to your local radio station, and *voila!*

Your favorite song was playing or probably would be within that hour, and you attentively listened so you would not miss it when the DJ let your tune spin.

Back then, if you wanted to hear a song on-demand, you had to get to a record shop, buy the record, bring it home and play it on your stereo. That was as on-demand as you could get for that time.

Radio stations were under the mistaken belief that they could stem the tide of people away from watching so much TV. At one time, radio had been the undisputed king of entertainment, but that was no longer the case.

In a valiant effort to gain new listeners and hang onto them, radio stations would run little contests. You know, the kind that would tell you to "Be caller number thirteen, and answer our question correctly, and you will win a..."

Our most local radio station was called KMEN – 129 in San Bernardino, California. And one day while I was listening, they ran a contest. It was 1965, I was innocent and 12 years old, and I was too excited for words. I was caller number thirteen, and now, for the first time in my life, I heard my voice on the radio! (I had no idea at the time that this foreshadowed things to come.)

So, the DJ said, "Ok, once again, our question is what famous musician was born in Liverpool, England?" I blurted out, "The Beatles!" The DJ could hear I was a kid, so he cut me some slack. "You are so close, but we are asking about one particular artist, not a group." I went blank. He continued to try to help me. "You have the right group, and our artist is a member of that group, so pick one of them." Of the Beatles, Paul McCartney was my favorite, and so that was my answer.

"You got it!" the DJ said. "You can come down to our station at any time in the next week and pick up your prize."

Man, I was jumping out of my skin! I could not wait until my mom or dad could drive me over to KMEN.

My mother drove me to the station, and I walked in, thinking I was going to pick whatever album I wanted out of their collection. I had high hopes of getting something from The Temptations, my favorite group at the time, but that was not to be.

They said to me, "You can have an album by this artist or by that artist, it's your choice."

When I came back to the car, my mom could see I had lost all my enthusiasm. She asked, "What happened?" I could see her maternal instincts kicking in, and she was about to get angry. If anyone had wronged her son in that radio station, they were about to pay—big time.

"They gypped me." (We were not as politically correct in the sixties as we should have been.) I continued, "They gave me a choice between two albums *they* picked. I never heard of either one of 'em, but I chose this one." I showed her the album. "You ever heard of this guy?" She glanced at the record, and she looked disappointed too. "Otis Redding? Nope," she answered.

When we got back home, I put the album on the stereo player and began to listen. My eyebrows raised, my mouth dropped open, and all I could say was, "Wow!"

The name of the album was *Otis Blue / Otis Redding Sings Soul*, and it was predominantly an album of *cover* songs; songs other artists had already done. But no one had ever heard them interpreted as Otis was doing here on this album. He truly made each song his own. I was stunned.

That album contained many great songs, including ones that would become hallmarks in Otis' career, like "I've Been Loving You Too Long (To Stop Now)," "Shake," "Satisfaction," and a little ditty called "Respect."

And even though all these songs became classics again with Otis singing them, the one I liked the most and started singing myself, was Otis' version of the Sam Cooke song, "A Change Is Gonna Come." And, not to sound sacrilegious, but I liked Otis' version better. It was so raw I could feel his emotions pummeling me. His voice was laced with lament and was so mournful you would have sworn he was at the funeral of his most beloved friend. It deeply impacted me, and I sing the song to this day.

Was I alone in my newfound belief that I had won a great album from K-MEN? Not by a long shot. Here is what *Wikipedia* says about *Otis Blue / Otis Redding Sings Soul*:

> The album was also ranked 74 on the 2003 *Rolling Stone* magazine's "500 Greatest Albums of All Time" list… It also ranked 92 on *Time* magazine's list of the "All-Time 100 Greatest Albums"… and [it was] included in *Q* magazine's "Best Soul Albums of All-Time" list… The album appeared in [the book] *1001 Albums You Must Hear Before You Die*. According to *Acclaimed Music, Otis Blue* is the 68th most frequently ranked record on critics' all-time lists. - https://bit.ly/2zVOYrE

I won at KMEN-129 with three guesses: The Beatles, Paul McCartney, and Otis Redding.

I'm with you, Lefty. I'd rather be lucky than good.

Just 24 months after Otis sang the mournful "A Change Is Gonna Come," he was killed in an airplane crash. He was only 26 years old.

The following videos of Otis Redding are rare, but one of them is the most extraordinary I have ever heard.

It is Otis singing "(Sitting On) The Dock of the Bay," with all the mistakes and miracles that we vocalists usually make in the studio on our first attempt to get our songs recorded for posterity. It is an incredible find.

***

Referenced Videos:

"I've Been Loving You
Too Long"
https://bit.ly/3gLnC85

"A Change Is Gonna Come"
https://bit.ly/3crYwIe

"(Sitting on) The Dock
of the Bay"
https://bit.ly/3gKln50

"Shake"
https://bit.ly/2ADYkbl

"Satisfaction"
https://bit.ly/2XqJ62s

Chapter 3 – Otis Blackwell

In 1991, I worked for a company named Pitney Bowes as a senior account executive, a fancy name for an outside sales representative.

When I had begun with the company four years earlier, I was an entry-level account representative, but over time, I worked my way up the ladder. I was appointed to represent my company in dealing with major accounts like Goodwill Industries, Aetna Insurance, and Director's Mortgage.

My local Pitney Bowes office was on Mount Vernon Avenue in Colton, California.

Colton, San Bernardino, Redlands, Loma Linda, and Highland California are neighboring cities, so if you have seen any of them, you will have a good idea about the area where I lived and worked.

My job was a tough gig, a grind, psychologically speaking. It paid on the straight commission plan. If you did not make your sales quota, you would be paid minimum wage, but not for long. Like most straight commission jobs, if you do not meet your quota a few times, you will be looking for other employment sooner rather than later.

And then, as it has forever been, the minimum wage was not enough to live on, and certainly not enough for a family of four, which is what we were at that time.

Still, you cannot control when a deal closes. No matter how hard you work, the sales you make rarely happen when you want or need them to, and major account deals always took longer to close than anticipated.

I had things in the pipeline ready to happen. But this pay period was going to be a minimum wage payday, and, as I returned home from work this particular afternoon, my mind was scrambling, trying to figure out what to do to make ends meet.

I was not having a good day, but I could not let my wife or children know that. I was worried enough for all of us. I never wanted them to have to worry about anything. I walked in the door of my home with a smile on my face that most certainly did not reflect the turmoil I was feeling inside.

But in the next five minutes, my life was going to change—forever.

After greeting everyone, the phone rang.

I heard a voice on the other end, ask, "Did you know that you have a hit record in Europe?" I was confused. I looked at the phone, then put it back to my ear. "What?" was the best response I could manage at the time.

The entertainment attorney, Martin Cohen, calling from Hollywood, changed his question into a statement. "You have a hit record in Europe. It's close to the end of the year, and we were wondering if you would like a ten thousand dollar advance in royalties?"

First, $10,000 was close to one-third of my annual income with Pitney Bowes back then. Figuring out how I was going to make ends meet that month immediately became a moot point. So, there was that.

But I had not written a song in 15 years, which was about the last time I had heard from Mr. Cohen. I had no idea what he was talking about, and my mind was reeling.

He continued, "A group called Incognito in London has covered one of your songs, 'Always There,' and it is doing very well."

And, just like that, the world changed.

In time, I had two hit songs. But my co-written tunes were not even in the same ballpark as those written by Otis Blackwell.

You may never have heard my songs "Always There" or "Such A Good Feeling," but I'd be willing to bet you have listened to the songs, "Don't Be Cruel," "All Shook Up," and "Return to Sender," recorded by Elvis Presley, right?

And if I asked you to name the signature song of the Music Hall of Fame artist, Jerry Lee Lewis, you would immediately say, "Great Balls of Fire."

If I asked you to name some of your favorite songs by James Taylor, "Handy Man" may be on your list.

And "Fever," a gold record by Little Willie John and an even bigger hit for Peggy Lee, is another iconic tune.

All of these are a part of the over one thousand songs written by Otis Blackwell, an African American singer/songwriter credited by music authorities as being a significant influence at the birth of what is now called rock and roll.

Here is something else about Blackwell that I found to be informative and revealing. An article in *Rolling Stone* magazine entitled "100 Greatest Songwriters of All Time" stated:

> And even though Blackwell's singing career never took off, it's been noted that his vocals on demos of songs that Presley recorded were followed faithfully by the King. "At certain tempo, the way Elvis sang was the result of copying Otis' demos," said Blackwell's friend Doc Pomus. - https://bit.ly/3dzG9CA

Now, how about that? The King's vocal style was probably influenced by a singer whose voice most of us have never heard.

Take a brief trip down memory lane with some great songs written by Otis Blackwell.

Something tells me that he had very few minimum wage paydays.

***

Referenced Videos:

"All Shook Up"
Elvis Presley
https://bit.ly/3eJVsZh

"Great Balls of Fire"
Jerry Lee Lewis
https://bit.ly/3eJVuQT

"Handy Man"
James Taylor
https://bit.ly/2U8tZc6

"Fever"
Peggy Lee
https://bit.ly/3gKmhhU

Chapter 4 – Hiroshima

In the early 1970s, Wayne Henderson, a founding member of the legendary Jazz Crusaders, became one of the most sought-after producers in music. He would discover talent, sign them to his company, At Home Productions, take them into the studio and produce an album for them, and then offer the product and the group to a major record company.

One day when I was in Hollywood, I bumped into Wayne on Sunset Blvd. He said to me, "If you'd like to drop by S.I.R. today around two o'clock, I've got a new group I'm trying to get signed to a record label. There will be reps from several record companies there to hear them. Come and check it out." S.I.R. (Studio Instrument Rentals) is a famous place among musicians. Instrument rental and rehearsal space for bands and a large room with a stage to showcase new acts are all available there for a price. At times you may see mega-stars there, like Stevie Wonder, etc.

Hanging out with Wayne opened so many doors for me that I would have never walked through on my own. The music scene is like an onion. It has many layers. Wayne peeled many of those layers back for me, so I got an upfront and personal view of how the music industry works.

"Sure! I'll be there," I replied.

I was excited. Wayne was known for discovering some of the funkiest bands of the time.

Groups like Pleasure and Black Smoke, and vocal artists like Side Effect, Miki Howard, David Oliver, and the super funky cousin of Bobby Womack, named Johnny Reasons, were all his protegees.

(The first time I heard Johnny, I got goosebumps. His voice and the songs he writes have an incredible drive. They can also be beautiful. Case in point, a song that Johnny and I co-wrote called "For You," which was recorded by Wayne on his *Emphasized* album and by one of Stevie Wonder's favorite female vocalists, Linda McCrary. The McCrary's album was called *All Night Music*.)

Then, Wayne had jazz artists too, like Ronnie Laws, Bobby Lyle, and Roland Bautista. So, I knew I was about to hear some greatness in just a couple of hours.

I arrived at S.I.R. at the appointed time, and I took a seat. There were several reps from many different companies there. I felt like I was the only civilian in the joint, just a lucky guy who got to be there and listen. I was the fly on the wall.

The band came out, all the members dressed in traditional Japanese garb. A huge taiko drum dominated the stage. I saw wooden flutes, and several other traditional Japanese musical instruments, including a koto, a stringed instrument reminiscent of a zither on steroids.

The band began to play traditional Japanese music. It was soft, lilting, and beautiful, but not at all what I had imagined I would hear when Wayne invited me.

I thought to myself, *Wayne has lost it! What is this?* I was genuinely flabbergasted. I looked around at the record company executives who were there. They seemed as puzzled as I did.

Suddenly, the traditional song they were playing morphed into something else. The bass guitar player started thumping and popping on the bass, announcing that something extraordinary was about to happen. Then the rest of the band kicked in. And when they did, I thought, *Oh, my God!*

Everyone in the place was immediately transfixed! The group was playing some of the funkiest music I had ever heard. I could not believe the groove of this predominately Japanese American band jamming in the 1970s. I wanted to stand up and shout. That transition—mid-song—was mind-blowing, and I could see that the record executives were now wholly engaged in the experience.

My, *Wayne has lost it,* turned into, *Wayne is a freakin' genius!*

But the best was yet to come. Few in the entire world had ever heard anything like what happened next.

June Kuramoto (wife of the group founder Dan Kuramoto), seated at the koto, began to play, and she made that instrument speak a new language.

Her fingers were flying as she played jazz riff after jazz rift, one flowing seamlessly into the next. Now I had to tie myself down to keep from standing and shouting praise as if I were in church.

June Kuramoto made jazz koto a thing. Her name and contribution to the world of jazz is her musical legacy. To this day, I have never heard anyone play the koto the way that she does. June Kuramoto is a musical genius.

Several of the record companies there that day jumped at the opportunity to sign this new group, Hiroshima, to their record label. Here is the origin of Hiroshima according to *Wikipedia*:

Dan Kuramoto, Hiroshima's leader, is from East Los Angeles. He attended California State University, Long Beach, then led its Asian-American studies department. Through playing in a band on weekends, he met June Kuramoto, a native of Japan who grew up in Los Angeles and played koto, a Japanese stringed instrument.

Kuramoto admired Earth, Wind, and Fire for the way it combined jazz and R&B, and Santana for his identification with Latinos. He wanted to create a band that would represent Asian Americans. He named it after the Japanese city Hiroshima, which was hit with a nuclear bomb during World War II.

Hiroshima's debut album sold more than 100,000 copies in its first three months. The band's second album yielded the song "Winds of Change," which received a Grammy Award nomination for Best R&B Instrumental. Hiroshima got its first gold album in 1985 with Another Place and the second with Go which followed it. The album Legacy was nominated for Best Pop Instrumental Album in 2010. Hiroshima has sold more than four million albums worldwide. In 1990, the band was the opening act for Miles Davis.

Hiroshima consists of Dan Kuramoto (saxophone, flute, keyboards, shakuhachi) June Kuramoto (koto), Kimo Cornwell (keyboards), Dean Cortez (bass guitar), and Danny Yamamoto (drums and taiko). - https://bit.ly/3dtBa61

Arista Records, the label run by Clive Davis (who discovered or boosted the careers of Santana, Janice Joplin, Earth, Wind & Fire, Sly and the Family Stone, and Whitney Houston, among others), won the bid for the services of Hiroshima.

I sincerely hope you will enjoy "One Wish" by Hiroshima, and if this is the first time you have ever listened to the jazz koto, you are in for a treat.

***

Referenced Videos:

"One Wish"
https://bit.ly/2Bkt4yv

Chapter 5 – Little Willie John

I met him when I was in the eighth grade of junior high school. I was fourteen years old and a little over five feet tall (approximately 162 centimeters). I towered over him by two or three inches (7.6 centimeters). He was 29 years old. There was no sarcasm intended when they called him Little Willie John. And, according to my parents, he was a star. He was the man who looked like a kid with a babyface whose voice was so powerful and soulful that you could not believe it was coming out of that small frame.

We were in Los Angeles, visiting my grandfather's brother, my great uncle Jimmy Allen. He and Little Willie John were friends, and Little Willie John happened to be visiting Uncle Jimmy and his wife, my Aunt Ruby, that same day.

I remember standing out on the balcony of my uncle's luxury apartment, talking with Little Willie John. He seemed to me to be a kind and friendly man. He did not talk down to me as if I were a child. The conversation was intelligent and funny, and my first impression was more than a favorable one.

Months later, I learned that this gentle, kind man was now in prison—for manslaughter.

The story goes that a woman sitting next to Little Willie John in a public venue had to go to the restroom, and she asked Little Willie John to save her seat.

A man, reportedly well over six feet tall and weighing about 250 pounds, tried to take the seat.

Bystanders said that Little Willie John politely explained to the man that he was holding the seat for the lady in the restroom. The man slammed his fist into Little Willie John's face so hard that it knocked him out of his chair and on to the floor.

When Willie got up, he had a knife in his hand, and that was that. (In those days, a lot of guys carried brass knuckles or knives or straight razors for protection. Being of such small stature, I can only guess that Willie probably took some form of protection with him everywhere he went. Again, I am guessing as I have never read where he got the knife that he used. But I do remember how things were back in the day.)

Sometime after his incarceration, I learned that Little Willie John was dead. He died under "mysterious circumstances," while a prisoner.

Have you never heard of Little Willie John?

How about James Brown? Well, he used to open for Little Willie John. If you know music or have been to concerts, you know what that means. The lesser act opens for the more popular one. James Brown was Little Willie John's opening act. Can you imagine James Brown warming up the audience for you?

And James Brown had such deep respect for his friend, that after Willie's death, Mr. Brown did a tribute album called *Thinking About Little Willie John and a few Nice Things.*

You may not have heard much about Little Willie John because he died so incredibly young. He was just 30 years old when he met his end in prison. He did have two gold singles before he died. There was "Talk to Me," and his other million-seller became an even bigger hit for an artist named Peggy Lee. The name of that song is "Fever."

Still, no one has ever sung "Fever" the way Little Willie John did on the original version.

I share that version with you today.

One final note. The world is an exceedingly small place. Fifties rock and roll legend Johnny Otis ("Willie and the Hand Jive") was the one who discovered Little Willie John and launched his career in the music business. Eight years after the night I met Little Willie John, Johnny Otis helped me record my first songs, one of which started my career in the music industry.

Enjoy the phenomenal voice of Little Willie John. He was utterly amazing.

***

Referenced Videos:

"Talk to Me"
https://bit.ly/3eFi1hG

"Fever"
https://bit.ly/3dFTLw9

Chapter 6 – Nana Mouskouri

Who is the most prolific musical artist of all time? Perhaps Elvis, Madonna, Beyoncé, Lady Gaga, or Taylor Swift come to mind. I mean, Elvis released a mind-blowing 78 albums while he was still alive.

But Elvis and all the rest pale in comparison to the beautiful Greek songstress known around the world as Nana Mouskouri.

Nana has released an estimated 450 albums and in 15 different languages. My vote for the most prolific artist in history goes to her.

Let us put this in perspective. LPs (pronounced El Peas, an abbreviation for long-playing records, a nickname for albums) typically contained about 45 minutes worth of music.

That would mean if you had each of Nana's albums and played them back to back, 24 hours a day, it would take you two weeks to hear them all; 14 days and nights non-stop, never hearing the same song twice.

In addition to her native language of Greek, Nana fluently speaks French, English, Spanish, Italian, and Portuguese.

How good is Nana? Quincy Jones himself convinced Nana to come to New York from Europe to record a jazz LP.

Quincy produced a beautiful album of standards, jazz, and soul, called Nana Mouskouri In New York.

The LP includes one of my favorite songs of all time, "Smoke Gets in Your Eyes."

Below, I am featuring "Smoke" and two other songs that Nana did as duets.

One with Harry Belafonte and the other with Julio Iglesias. They are both beautiful as well.

Nana worked closely with legendary composer, Michael Legrand, and the result was two hit records in France.

In between recording all these albums, Nana somehow found time to get married, have two children, and host a TV show for nearly ten years.

At eighty-four years old, Nana is still active, and why not? She has only sold 300 million albums. Just between you and me, I think the woman is a slacker.

Enjoy the videos of this great artist who is truly the hardest working woman in show business.

***

Referenced Videos:

"Smoke Gets in Your Eyes"
https://bit.ly/2EtrGLP

"Try to Remember"
Nana Mouskouri &
Harry Belafonte
https://bit.ly/3054ATW

"La Paloma"
Nana Mouskouri
& Julio Iglesias
https://bit.ly/2Xs1sjL

Chapter 7 – Johnny & Shuggie Otis

My father and I stood there, just outside of Johnny's studio. It was a separate building located in the backyard of Johnny's large home in Los Angeles, California. This property was like nothing I had ever seen before.

To get to the studio, we had to pass over a small pond filled with what Johnny called Koi fish. I thought, *Man, these are some humongous goldfish!*

That was the day my horizons began to expand, and they would eventually widen far beyond my wildest dreams. But it was 1973. I was 20 years old, feeling very uneasy, and wondering where in the world Johnny had found these freakishly large, multi-colored monstrosities. Those mutated goldfish were beginning to freak me out.

Johnny looked at my father and me and said, "Yes, I have some great musicians from Las Vegas for your session. We have a drummer, keyboard player, and bass player. But we don't need a guitar player, because we have Shuggie" (an affectionate alteration of the word sugar, like calling him "little sugar").

Shuggie was Johnny's son, a handsome, free-spirited, guitar-playing musical prodigy, who was a few months younger than me.

The genius that Shuggie possesses is genetic. His father, Johnny, is a musical icon.

Here is what *Wikipedia* says about Johnny:

Johnny Otis (born Ioannis Alexandres Veliotes; December 28, 1921 – January 17, 2012) was an American singer, musician, composer, arranger, bandleader, talent scout, disc jockey, record producer, television show host, artist, author, journalist, minister, and impresario. He was a seminal influence on American R&B and rock and roll. He discovered numerous artists early in their careers who went on to become highly successful in their own right, including Little Esther Phillips, Etta James, Big Mama Thornton, Johnny Ace, Jackie Wilson, Little Willie John, Hank Ballard, and The Robins (who eventually changed their name to The Coasters), among many others. Otis has been called the original "King of Rock and Roll" and the "Godfather of Rhythm and Blues." – https://bit.ly/2XSTqPX

Johnny was about to help me become discovered too.

"We have Shuggie." Johnny had said. He continued, "We can have him lay down some chink guitar."

The term political correctness was decades away from being used by the general population; still, I cringed when he said that. Maybe Johnny caught my expression. He started to laugh. Then he acted as if he were playing the guitar.

"You know," he said as he dragged his imaginary pick over the imaginary strings of his imaginary guitar, "on the two (the second beat of a measure), and the four (the fourth beat of a measure), all Shuggie has to do is play chink. Chink. Chink. Chink."

I got it, and I had to smile. No, Johnny Otis was not a closet racist, after all. Chink was an onomatopoeia, not a racial slur. I felt so much better.

Johnny, along with my arranger Frank Kavelin, produced my first four songs (as demo records).

The songs turned out so well that the moment Side Effect heard one of the songs, they chose to record it on their first album with Fantasy Records. The name of that song is "Baby Love (Love You Baby)." I am proud to say that the bass player on that song recorded by Side Effect was Louis Johnson of The Brothers Johnson. My career as a songwriter was born. That led to becoming a vocalist, a recording artist, and then, the lead vocalist of one of the most significant groups in musical history, the Platters.

Johnny is no longer with us, but his uber-talented son, Shuggie, is still thrilling audiences everywhere with his virtuosity. He is a Blues Man, first and foremost. Back in the days when I met him, he was writing songs like the enigmatic "Strawberry Letter 23," which would become a major hit for The Brothers Johnson.

Wow! In all these years, I just now see a connection I have never noticed before. The Brothers Johnson sang and played Shuggie's song, and half of that group played on my first song for Side Effect, and it was Shuggie who played on the original demo of that song. Man, life is a trip. If the Otis family had not been the subject of *The Saturday Morning Song Chronicles* this weekend, I would never have made that connection. Amazing.

The video playlist today will have the iconic 1950s hit by Johnny Otis, called "Willie and the Hand Jive," and also the song that Shuggie wrote, which became a hit for The Brothers Johnson, "Strawberry Letter 23." But I am going to share with you Shuggie's original version of that song.

The final video will be of Side Effect performing my song "Baby Love (Love You Baby)."

I was proud to have Side Effect choose this song for their album, and I could not have been more pleased to have the great Shuggie Otis play chink guitar on the demo version.

Another blessing was having musicians like Louis Johnson, Arthur Adams, and George Bohannon play the music on my first published, recorded song. It was an auspicious beginning for me.

***

Referenced Videos:

"Willie and the Hand Jive"
Johnny Otis
https://bit.ly/2ADn83a

"Strawberry Letter 23"
Shuggie Otis
https://bit.ly/2MrpAg5

"Baby Love (Love You Baby)
Side Effect
https://bit.ly/2MluOtE

Chapter 8 – Soulful Voices

I saw a video once where a tough gang-banger was harassing an older man on a bus. Someone with a camera phone recorded the whole thing. The older man, trying to maintain peace, got up, walked to the front of the bus, and took an empty seat.

The buff gang-banger followed him up to the front of the bus and then proceeded to put his hands on the older man. The older guy had enough. He stood up, punched the bully in the face one time, and the bully hit the floor, knocked out cold. Everyone on the bus applauded. I did too.

I was watching a David versus Goliath story, and upon seeing this video, I smiled, shook my head, and said, "You can never judge a book by its cover."

That same maxim holds in music.

I believe that everybody has soul, the expression of which is as unique as the person is. Anthony Hamilton has soul, but so does Yo-Yo Ma.

Case in point, I would like to share some of my favorite soulful voices with you today, all singing songs that have touched my life in one way or another. But notice that these are not songs by Otis Redding, or Keb Mo, or the Temptations, or Aretha Franklin, or Gladys Knight. Those artists are some of my favorites, but they are not the ones I am sharing with you today.

No, instead, the soulful voices I present to you today have names like Dusty Springfield, Chris Stapleton, Len Berry, and Bobby Hatfield and Bill Medley of the Righteous Brothers. There is even a guy named Ji-hwan, who is a member of the group 2Bic in South Korea, and when he sings, I get a lump in my throat and tears well in my eyes. His may be one of the most soulful, pleasing, and disciplined voices of our time.

If there is one take-away from *The Saturday Morning Song Chronicles* this a.m., I hope it is this. When it comes to soulful voices, you can never judge a book by its cover.

Enjoy these rare and historical videos, and I hope to see you back here again next week for the next installment of *The Saturday Morning Song Chronicles*.

***

Referenced Videos:

"Heaven" – 2BiC
https://bit.ly/2yYAeaV

"Son of a Preacher Man"
Dusty Springfield
https://bit.ly/39zzYwQ

"(You're My) Soul and
Inspiration"
The Righteous Brothers
https://bit.ly/3eII1Zz

"1-2-3" – Len Barry
https://bit.ly/3dvsv37

"Tennessee Whiskey"

Chapter 9 – James Brown

When I began *The Saturday Morning Song Chronicles* on James Brown, I was stunned to learn that he was one of the most prolific musical artists of all time. He recorded hit songs for fifty-one years, starting in 1956 and recording until 2007. In his lifetime James Brown recorded 129 albums. One of his nearest male competitors was Elvis, who recorded about 78 albums.

My grandfather, Paul B Allen, Sr., booked James Brown into his club, Allen's Showcase, in Omaha, Nebraska, back in the late 1950s and early 1960s. Because of the racial issues of the day, many black entertainers, like Fats Domino and James Brown, resided at my grandfather's house during their tour in Omaha. Often, Mr. Brown would be picked up at the airport by my Uncle Alfred Allen, or my great uncle Jesse Allen. According to all reports, Mr. Brown felt like he was treated well by the Allen family.

I never noticed James Brown until he recorded "Papa's Got A Brand New Bag" in 1964. I was just an 11-year-old kid then.

The music of James Brown was different, and that song, "Papa's Got a Brand New Bag," featured "syncopation" like nothing before it ever had. He was crafting a new genre in music that would come to be called funk music.

The thing that kills me is that the album that this song came from was James Brown's eleventh studio album!

"Say It Loud – I'm Black and I'm Proud" one of his biggest hits ever, was his twenty-seventh studio album, and there were many more to come.

Yes, we could talk about his being one of the first black men to own a series of radio stations, or that he purchased a private jet to get to his gigs more quickly or that he owned the master recordings of his music which was unheard of in the record industry at that time.

We could also talk about the fact that James Brown, like Maurice White of Earth, Wind & Fire, and Marvin Gaye, also started as a drummer before becoming a lead vocalist.

But I began *The Saturday Morning Song Chronicles* about James Brown with only one thing in mind. In his style of singing, Mr. Brown would scream and shout so emotively that it became his trademark vocal style, and decades later, musicians still sample his music and his voice.

However, what I wanted you to hear today is a song that showcases the fact that James Brown had a fantastic, high voice before he started doing so very much shouting in his songs. As a singer, I can assure you that screaming out a song wreaks havoc on your vocal cords and dramatically reduces your vocal range over time.

Please listen to this song James recorded back in 1963 called "Prisoner of Love." Hear how he glides so beautifully into notes. Listen to his extraordinary range and how he breathes raw power and emotion into every word. It still gives me chills every time I hear it. Enjoy "Prisoner of Love" from his seventh studio album and thank you for joining us here at *The Saturday Morning Song Chronicles*. See you next week.

***

Referenced Videos:

"Prisoner of Love"
https://bit.ly/3dttjph

Chapter 10 – Arthur Adams

Want to hear one of the funkiest bass solos ever? Listen to this short clip from a little-known single I co-wrote with a blues/funk guitarist/bassist by the name of Arthur Adams.

Once upon a time, Wayne Henderson of the Crusaders called me and asked me to meet with Arthur, an artist he was producing. Arthur had a great music track, and Wayne wanted me to help with the lyrics of the song. So, I met Arthur at his home in Los Angeles.

Arthur was so humble and genuinely kind that I liked him immediately. I had no idea what a musical heavyweight he was. I thought he was a new artist Wayne was producing, and Arthur's manner and style never led me to believe otherwise.

He liked the lyrics I wrote for his song, called "Fire."

Why do I say that Arthur is a heavyweight in the world of music? His industry credits tell the tale.

Along with being a solo artist, songwriter, and fronting his band, Arthur was also a full-time studio session musician. These guys are musician's musicians, some of the top players in the entire music industry.

How good is Arthur Adams? The answer becomes apparent when you look at who paid him top dollar to play on their recording projects. Here is a short list:

Quincy Jones (80 Grammy nominations and 28 Grammy wins). Henry Mancini (72 Grammy nominations and 20 Grammy wins). Lou Rawls (13 Grammy nominations and 3 Grammy wins). Nancy Wilson (7 Grammy nominations and 3 Grammy wins). The Jackson 5 (2 Grammy nominations), Sonny Bono (2 Grammy nominations). Willie Hutch (1 Grammy nomination). And the Vegas mainstays who recorded a significant soul hit called "Black Pearl," Sonny Charles & The Checkmates. Arthur played in that session too.

Artists of this caliber hire only the absolute best musicians to be on their projects. They could choose anyone in the world to play for them. They all chose Arthur Adams.

I classified this as the short list because Arthur has performed on hundreds of recording sessions.

He also contributed to TV and movie soundtracks, including *Cactus Flower, Buck and the Preacher, The Bill Cosby Show, and Ironside.* His song "Love and Peace" was covered by Quincy Jones on Quincy's Grammy award-winning 1969 album *Walking in Space.*

In 1981 Arthur had a solo hit called "You Got the Floor," which reached number 1 on the U.K. disco chart that year and 38 on the U.K. singles chart.

Arthur wrote two songs, which appeared on B.B. King's 1992 album, *There Is Always One More Time.* And Arthur became a bandleader at B. B. King's blues club in Los Angeles, often performing with drummer James Gadson.

Adams recorded a version of Ann Peebles' soul classic "I Can't Stand the Rain" for the movie *Town and Country*, starring Goldie Hawn (mother of actress Kate Hudson). He also performed at the Saint Louis Blues Heritage Festival in August 1997, and in November at the Utrecht Blues Estafette in The Netherlands.

So, here I was, 23 years old, thinking I'm hot stuff and helping a new artist with his lyrics. And Arthur was so cool that he never let on that he was one of the most coveted musicians in the world. The truth was that, as the old folks used to say, I was not even a "pimple on his behind."

At the time, I thought the coolest thing about this situation was that Arthur recorded on an independent record label that belonged to actor Bernie Hamilton, who played the police captain on the original Starsky and Hutch TV show.

That small independent record label went defunct shortly after Arthur recorded our song, "Fire." As a result, that tune has virtually disappeared over time.

Here is a clip of the original eight-minute disco/dance/jazz version of the song. The radio version was closer to three minutes. This clip, which features that super-funky bass solo I was telling you about in the beginning, is one of the things that makes this cut so noteworthy and will be of interest to bass players all around the world. Another point of musical interest is that the fabulous vocal group, Side Effect, sang the background vocals on this track.

Also included in today's video is my favorite Arthur Adams tune, "Home Brew." Those in the know say that the legendary bass player of the Funk Brothers, James Jamerson, is playing bass on this track. And, of course, Arthur is lighting it up.

Enjoy and marvel at the astounding creativity of this soulful, funky, musician of musicians, Arthur Adams.

***

Referenced Videos:

"Fire"
https://bit.ly/30VB1n9

"Homebrew"
https://bit.ly/2Xu5VCt

Chapter 11 – Darrell Banks

It turns out I had pretty good taste in music when I was a little kid. Case in point? Just yesterday I read this in *Wikipedia*: "In December 2014 collectors were bidding many thousands of pounds [in this case $24,000], for a copy of "Open the Door to Your Heart" in an online auction held in the UK." - https://bit.ly/2U3nZ44

The first record I ever purchased with my own money as a youngster was "Open the Door to Your Heart," by Darrell Banks. I heard it on the radio, hopped on my bike and pedaled the three to four miles to a store called White Front, in San Bernardino, California, and bought the album that featured that song. It cost me $3.49. High finance when my allowance was a buck a week.

This discovery of Darrell Banks happened around the time I had decided I wanted to teach myself how to sing. I was insulted and embarrassed at being rejected by the director of the Chorus Class at Mill Elementary School. He felt I was not good enough to be a member.

Anyway, I listened to "Open the Door to Your Heart" a million times, and I learned to sing it. I sounded "fair to middling," as the old folks used to say, but even that was enough for me to spawn a most radical idea. I thought to myself for the very first time, *Maybe one day I could be a real singer too!*

As bright a future as I thought Darrell Banks would have, I never heard any more of his songs, and I wondered what had become of him over the years.

I learned that he died just 48 months after recording "Open the Door to Your Heart." It turns out that he was "killed" by an off-duty policeman.

What happened? After piecing the story together, here is what 2+2 added up to in my mind.

It appears that Darrell and his girlfriend were having problems. He waited outside of her home (maybe all night?), but she arrived at 11 a.m. in a car with another man. She got out of the vehicle, and Darrell walked up to her (imagine the look on her face). Darrell took her by the arm and said, "We need to talk."

The guy she was with then identified himself as an off-duty cop, and he told Darrell to let go of her. And here is where the story gets dodgy.

Allegedly, when Darrell heard that he was dealing with the law, he pulled a gun from his waistband and pointed it at the off-duty cop. So, according to the story, the policeman said he got out of the line of fire, pulled his gun and shot Darrell dead.

Sound strange? It gets stranger. Not until eight days later was Darrell's death reported.

What was the cop doing with Darrell's girlfriend in the first place? Like that reported account, it sounds like some shenanigans were afoot.

Still, the bottom line is that Darrell died at 33 years of age, and I will always feel that this was a terrible loss on many different levels. Musically, I am certain Darrell Banks had years of hits to share with us, but now they have been lost forever.

At any rate, many in the world who love sweet soul music recognize that Darrell Banks was an extraordinary talent, and to get that last known vinyl recording of "Open The Door To Your Heart" was well worth the $24,000 paid for it at auction.

If you look below this article, you will find a link to an excellent YouTube video featuring Darrel Banks and that great song.

One final note. If the music to this song sounds a little "Motown-ish" that would be because an estimated 85%-90% of the musicians on this record were from the Motown band called The Funk Brothers who played on nearly every single hit record from Motown you have ever heard, at least up to about 1972.

The Funk Brothers often played on tracks for other artists around Detroit. However, they used pseudonyms, or would not be credited at all, so that Berry Gordy would not discover they were moonlighting.

I have only one question. Where the heck is my copy of "Open the Door to Your Heart" now? I never throw anything away. It has got to be around here somewhere...

***

Referenced Videos:

"Open the Door to Your Heart"
https://bit.ly/2XrJPAn

Chapter 12 – Hubert Laws

It is rare to find a musician with a dance music/ R&B instrumental hit song who is also a world-renowned classical musician who has played Carnegie Hall. But that is the caliber of musician you will find in Hubert Laws. Hubert plays Bach one moment, then moves on to dance music or funk/jazz music, as his latest song, "I Tell Thestory" will demonstrate.

The Chicago Theme is an album by this great flutist recorded at the legendary Rudy Van Gelder's Studio in New Jersey in 1974 and released in 1975 on the CTI label (Creed Taylor Incorporated). It climbed to number eight on *Billboard* magazine's Disco/Dance Tracks chart in 1975.

On *Billboard's* R&B chart, where his siblings Ronnie, Eloise, and Debra would also later have hits, the flute-based instrumental made it to #53. Every adventure TV show of that time copied licks (musical phrases) from this song to incorporate into their TV theme songs.

As noted above, Hubert is part of a tremendously talented musical family. His sisters Eloise and Debra are both professional vocalists, and his brother, Ronnie, played saxophone with Earth, Wind & Fire before going solo. With Wayne Henderson of the Crusaders producing, Ronnie recorded the incredible, fastest-selling debut album in the history of Blue Note Records, called *Pressure Sensitive*.

But long before Eloise and Debra and Ronnie made a significant impact on the world of music, Hubert was already recognized as one of the finest flutists in the world.

Today, I present three songs to you to demonstrate how incredibly skilled this musician is. You will hear him play a piece written by Johann Sabastian Bach, followed by the dance hit song Hubert released in 1975, called "Chicago Theme (Love Loop)," and finally, his very latest song, produced in 2019. This song is by Opolopo, the noted musician/producer from Hungary. I believe that the very cool, "I Tell Thestory" is going to do well on the *Billboard* magazine charts.

I had the honor of meeting Hubert one day, and here is how it went. I extended my hand. "Hi, I'm Paul Allen. I co-wrote 'Always There' with your brother, Ronnie." Hubert nodded as we shook hands—and that was that. I look back and laugh now. It occurs to me that Hubert is a sensitive and quiet man who lets his gargantuan skill speak on his behalf.

Check out his virtuosity and mastery of multiple musical genres as *The Saturday Morning Song Chronicles* salutes Mr. Hubert Laws.

***

Referenced Videos:

J.S. Bach "Sonata 5 e minor"
Hubert Laws
David Budway
https://bit.ly/2AwftUC

"The Chicago Theme (Love Loop)
https://youtu.be/Fpj-fk3rdLw

"I Tell Thestory"
Opolopo
Hubert Laws

Spoken Word: Gregory Porter

https://bit.ly/2BFz6ua

Chapter 13 – LTD

LTD (Love, Togetherness, and Devotion), was one of the most underrated bands of the '70s. They had a sense of musical style and elegance that many groups of that time did not have.

They also had Jeffrey Osborne. That was the blessing and the curse of LTD.

It was a blessing because Osborne (a drummer who became the lead singer, much like Maurice White and Marvin Gaye had been) had a style of singing that was uniquely his but fit perfectly with the music the band was creating.

LTD had landmark ballads, some of the most danceable music of the day, and they even had Funk songs. This band was dynamic, yet sensitive and nuanced. The music they created was infectious, fun, uniquely engaging, and always done in a different way than others were doing it, and in a different way than your ear would expect to hear.

There were Easter eggs hidden in their songs. Just listen, and you will hear their music zig left when you were sure it was about to zag right, and that deliciously executed surprise makes you smile. Check out their funk tune "Jam" and feel the delight when the chorus comes and spins you off into another direction.

Osborne's voice was the thread that held it all together through their hits like "Holding On," "Back in Love Again," and "Love Ballad," all number one records on *Billboard's* R&B Chart.

That was the blessing of Jeffrey Osborne for LTD.

But the curse was when their super-vocalist Osborne left the group to pursue his inevitable solo career. And what success he achieved. His songs included "We're Going All the Way," "Stay with Me Tonight," and the mega-hit, "On the Wings of Love."

What do you do when the voice that is your very brand leaves? You bring in another singer who has a unique and powerful voice, which is what LTD did. They brought in a great singer that I have the pleasure of knowing, Leslie Wilson, formerly of the group New Birth (Leslie sang the hits "Wildflower" and "Dream Merchant"). Leslie helped LTD to a few more hit records before he left the group, but those hits did not approach the magnitude of the ones enjoyed with Osborne as the lead.

The magic that LTD and Jeffrey Osborne created together was forever lost: LTD would never become as big as Earth, Wind & Fire, or Tower of Power. And that is a shame because at their peak LTD was inspiring.

I share with you one of their most beautiful ballads (I think one of the prettiest songs of all time), called "We Both Deserve Each Other's Love." Also, in this four-song playlist that I have curated for you, you will find one of their infectiously quirky hits, "Back in Love Again." Another of my favorites, "Holding On," and "Jam," the funk song mentioned above as having the Easter egg chorus, is here too.

This band was different but different in an enchanting way.

Enjoy LTD, whose music even forty years later still sounds fresh, engaging, and relevant.

The Saturday Morning Song Chronicles salutes the band LTD.

***

Referenced Videos:

"Back in Love Again"
https://bit.ly/3gOtddY

"Holding On"
https://bit.ly/3dtrloZ

"We Both Deserve
Each Other's Love"
https://bit.ly/305c3CH

"Jam"
https://bit.ly/3jTYrSz

Chapter 14 – Tower of Power

No, the phenomenal Lenny Williams was not the first lead vocalist of Tower of Power (TOP), but his voice is the one most of us associate with the group, even though his time with them was only about two years.

In their first album, released in 1970 and named *East Bay Grease*, TOP featured not one, but two different lead vocalists.

The first was a singer named Rufus Miller. His voice was gravelly and powerful but sounds foreign when you think of the Tower of Power sound today.

By all accounts, however, he was a fantastic guy, well-loved by all. The song he sang that started getting TOP a little traction was "Knock Yourself Out." It is the first song I curated for your Tower of Power video list today, which holds all the songs mentioned in this article.

The second featured vocalist on that first album was named Rick Stevens. Rick had a higher and prettier voice. He sang a song called "Sparkling in the Sand," and that song got much more radio play and real traction for the group.

So, between their first album and the second, Rufus Miller left the group.

Their second album, released in 1972, *Bump City* (the group's first with their new record label Warner Brothers), featured only one vocalist, Rick Stevens. The new album had two hits. "Down to the Nightclub," and the song that put TOP on my radar, "You're Still a Young Man." Oh my goodness, I loved that song.

I remember seeing Rick on one or two TV shows performing with the group, but just as "You're Still a Young Man," was climbing the charts, Rick disappeared. I can't tell you why, exactly, but I can tell you this. Not long after leaving the group, Rick murdered three people in a drug deal gone wrong. He was given life in prison but released after serving 36 years. He died a couple of years after being released, but in between those events, Rick returned to entertaining, and I am sharing a video of him performing "You're Still A Young Man" to a live audience. It brought tears to my eyes.

Tower of Power had their biggest album ever the next year, 1973, with the eponymous *Tower of Power*.

For this album, TOP hired Lenny Williams as their new lead vocalist, and suddenly, there was magic! Lenny sang "This Time It's Real," my personal favorite, "What Is Hip," and the most significant single in their history, "So Very Hard to Go."

A lot was happening in the group that facilitated all that creativity just then. Not only did Williams join the group at that time, but also the great horn player Lenny Pickett, who would spin and dance as he played in a way that no one else had done before. His dancing added a fantastic visual to the group. (Lenny Pickett went on to become the Musical Director of the long-running TV show *Saturday Night Live*.)

Also, joining the group at that time was perhaps the funkiest organ player in history, Chester Thompson. Thompson's organ solos are legend.

And replacing the original guitar player was the dynamic Bruce Conte. Bruce's guitar solos and riffs played a significant part in forming the sound of TOP. (Bruce and I met and spent some time together nearly 20 years ago. He loves the Blues more than any other kind of music, and when he takes a break from playing with TOP, which he frequently does, he forms a little Blues group and performs at smaller, more intimate venues. I believe we met when he was playing the Suncoast in Las Vegas.)

These new members, now paired with the established members of TOP, made it the most exciting band to watch and to hear of any group out there. They led the way for larger bands like Earth, Wind & Fire to follow.

Before I close, allow me to share a personal story with you.

Gene McDaniels, an international star vocalist and dear friend of my grandfather and father, came to visit our family when we moved to California. I believe he was living in the Skyforest area of the mountains in San Bernardino County. Gene had million-selling records and was a great songwriter (Remember "Feel Like Making Love" by Roberta Flack?). He was also a producer.

I remember Gene telling us that night that he was about to produce Lenny Williams, who had just left this group called Tower of Power. I listened as he described Lenny to my parents. Gene said that Lenny was "a really good guy," and Gene further expressed how impressive Lenny was as a person.

He explained that when Lenny spent a week or so with him and his family as the two began brainstorming the new album, Lenny made his bed every morning before he left his bedroom and was always a perfect gentleman.

He also said that Lenny did not like drugs or felt that TOP was so into drugs that it was detrimental, and that this was one of the primary reasons he left the group.

The guys in Tower of Power will tell you today that they were hard rockers, doing what most hard rockers were doing in those days; drugs were the norm, not the exception. But listening to what Gene had to say about him made my respect for Lenny shoot beyond the stratosphere. To leave one of the most popular musical groups in history after helping them get their biggest hits? It had to do with his stellar moral compass. He refused to condone the things he was seeing happening around him, and with courage, he took action.

No, the phenomenal Lenny Williams was not the first lead vocalist of Tower of Power. However, his voice is the one that will forever be associated with that force of nature, which is still rolling nearly 50 years later with the sound and style forged way back in 1973.

***

Referenced Videos:

"Knock Yourself Out"
(Lead: Rufus Miller)
https://bit.ly/3csx399

"Sparkling in the Sand"
(Lead: Rick Stevens)
https://bit.ly/3eLF7Dq

"Down to the Nightclub"
(Lead: Rick Stevens)
https://bit.ly/36VCTyJ

"You're Still a Young Man"
(Lead: Rick Stevens
performing live)
https://bit.ly/3gOtLQS

"This Time It's Real"
(Lead: Lenny Williams live
on Soul Train)
https://bit.ly/3cvKWmU

"What Is Hip"
(Lead: Lenny Williams)
https://bit.ly/3eXuD4f

"So Very Hard to Go"
(Lead: Lenny Williams)
https://bit.ly/2XW5DmT

Chapter 15 – Luther Vandross

My friends often laugh at me. If I enjoy something, I will say, "Man, this is the best in the world," as in "Man, this is the best burrito in the world," or "Man, this is the greatest TV show in the world." What can I say? I love what I love.

Something must be the best in its category, right? For instance, there is a burrito out there that is the best in the world. My vote goes to Amapola Mexican Restaurant in San Bernardino, California. There you will find the Chili Verde Burrito, but whatever you do, make yours an all-meat burrito because the rice and beans take up space where another couple of chunks of that delicious pork stewed in chili verde salsa could have been.

For my money, I say that I love Stevie Wonder, and Donny Hathaway, and Jeffery Osborne and Peabo Bryson, and Will Downing, and James Ingram and Brian McKnight and Lenny Williams and Howard Hewitt and Phil Perry. I even like that Paul B Allen III guy, although his name has no right to be mentioned in the same breath as any of the artists spoken of above. Still, I like him. What can I tell you?

But here's the thing. None of these singers get my vote for the best vocalist in the world. There is one man who does, and in my opinion, that man is Luther Vandross.

We could talk about his superior technical skills and his vocal gymnastics. We could talk about the timbre of his voice, which made it so beautiful and unique. We could talk about how warm and recognizable his voice was.

Before Luther hit the scene, I heard a commercial on TV. It was for the US Army, and someone was singing, "Be all that you can be." That voice made me freeze in my tracks, literally, and I thought, *Oh, my God, who is this singer?* I stood there, slack-jawed and thinking that someone new was about to conquer the world. I had never heard a voice more beautiful. I kept the TV on that station and sat and waited to listen to that commercial again. I told you, I love what I love.

When his first hit song was released, I knew beyond question that this guy singing "Never Too Much, " Luther Vandross, was the same guy I heard singing that Army commercial months earlier. That is what I mean when I say his voice was recognizable. I did not know his name when that commercial aired, but I would never forget that voice.

So, yes, we could talk about all these things.

But one aspect of Mr. Vandross that rarely gets taken into consideration when talking about what made him so excellent is how he "Luther-ized" songs. That is the term he coined for his process. He could take a song done well by someone else, and then launch it to stratospheric heights when he recorded it.

Case in point, the song "Never Let Me Go." It was a hit record back in the early 1950s by an ill-fated artist named Johnny Ace. After scoring eight hit records in a row within two years, Johnny accidentally shot himself in the head at the age of 25. (He will be the topic of *The Saturday Morning Song Chronicles* in the future.)

Anyway, Luther Vandross took what was a nearly 40-year-old hit record at that time, and he made it something so gorgeous that you would never even know it was the same song.

What he called Luther-izing his songs is a significant reason Mr. Vandross gets my vote.

Listen to "Never Let Me Go" by Johnny Ace, then listen to "Never Let Me Go," the Luther-ized version, and see one of the many reasons I firmly believe that Luther Vandross was the best male pop/R&B vocalist of our time.

***

Referenced Videos:

"Never Too Much"
Luther Vandross
https://bit.ly/3gOvg1E

"Never Let Me Go"
Johnny Ace
https://bit.ly/3eMsvMA

"Never Let Me Go"
Luther Vandross
https://bit.ly/305ttzo

Chapter 16 – Jesse Belvin

As my grandmother used to say to me when I was a child, "Fifty thousand Frenchmen can't be wrong, honey."

Where that saying comes from, I have no idea. I loved my grandmother, but between you, me, and the lamppost, Grandmother was a narcissist to the nth degree, and she was always referring to her good looks whenever she made this comment (which was often). Yet, to my knowledge, she had never actually been to France even once.

Still, her meaning was clear. If everyone is saying it, and everyone agrees with it, it (whatever it happens to be) is probably true.

From the time I began to sing in public, there is one word that people repeatedly used to describe my voice and vocal style, and that word is smooth. My dear friend, bass guitarist Derrick Murdock (*The Jay Leno Show* band), gave me the nickname T.J. Smooth and has been calling me that for two decades and counting.

I never recognized that I had this vocal quality until people like Derrick informed me that I did. At one point, I began to wonder if my grandmother's "fifty thousand Frenchmen" were trying to tell me something too.

Once I believed it (I was holding out for somebody, anybody, to describe my voice as sexy, not anything else), I wanted to figure out from where this smooth quality came.

I delved into my past.

When I was in the sixth grade of elementary school, I tried to join the school chorus. After testing me, the chorus teacher said in so many words, "Thanks, but no thanks." As a result, my embarrassment made me want to learn to sing, and now obviously, I was going to have to teach myself. (See my book From Karaoke to the Platters). I figured the best way to do that was to listen to others who were great singers.

I came across an album in my father's massive record collection, I listened, and I loved what I heard. The album was called *Mr. Easy*.

Nancy Wilson, Lou Rawls, and many others have called *Mr. Easy* the best pop album of all time.

The singer was Jesse Belvin. Smooth was the same word that most people used to describe his voice too.

My friends, I do not believe in reinventing the wheel.

Here is what *VintageMusicFm*, published on April 26, 2016, had to say about Jesse Belvin:

Jesse Lorenzo Belvin (December 15, 1932 – February 6, 1960) was an American R&B singer, pianist and songwriter popular in the 1950s, whose success was cut short by his death in a car crash aged 27.

Belvin was born in Texarkana, Texas, and moved with his family to Los Angeles at the age of five.

In 1950 he joined saxophonist Big Jay McNeely's backing vocal quartet, Three Dots and a Dash, and featured prominently on their record releases. In 1952 he joined Specialty Records. Although his early solo records were unsuccessful, his fourth record, "Dream Girl", credited to Jesse & Marvin and featuring Marvin Phillips on saxophone, reached number two on the R&B charts in 1953.

He was then drafted into the army but continued to write songs. His composition "Earth Angel", eventually co-credited to Belvin and Hollywood Flames singers Curtis Williams and Gaynel Hodge after a legal dispute was recorded by the Penguins and became one of the first R&B singles to cross over onto the pop charts, selling a million copies in 1954/55.

In 1956, he signed a contract with Modern Records but also continued to sing for other labels under different names. His biggest hit was "Goodnight My Love" which reached #7 on the R&B chart. 11-year-old Barry White reportedly played the piano on the session. The song became the closing theme to Alan Freed's rock and roll radio shows.

Belvin's other recordings for Modern were less successful, and in 1958 he recorded on Dot Records with a group, the Shields, who included lead singer Frankie Ervin and guitarist Johnny "Guitar" Watson. Their record, "You Cheated", reached #15 on the US pop chart and #11 on the R&B chart.

He also recorded with Eugene Church as the Cliques on a less successful single, "Girl of My Dreams" which was covered by the Four Lovers, two of whose members including Frankie Valli would later become the Four Seasons.

Inspired by his wife and manager Jo Ann to develop his style, he signed to RCA Records in 1959, and immediately had a Top 40 hit with "Guess Who", written by his wife. This song originally started as a love letter from her to him, and Belvin turned it into the hit song it became.

He also recorded an album, Just Jesse Belvin, developing a more mature and sophisticated sound on ballads. His style was influenced by Nat "King" Cole and Billy Eckstine and became a model for Sam Cooke and others. He acquired the nickname "Mr. Easy", and the record company began molding him as a potential crossover star for white audiences, as well as a professional rival to Capitol Records' recording star Nat "King" Cole.

He recorded a further series of tracks later in the year, with arranger Marty Paich and an orchestra including saxophonist Art Pepper. The songs included soulful covers of standards like "Blues in the Night", "In the Still of the Night", and "Makin' Whoopee", and were issued on the album Mr. Easy." – https://bit.ly/3cwZBhI

Here are a few songs from that magnificent *Mr. Easy* album that I learned by heart, word for word, note for note when I was twelve years old.

Now, decades later, I have come to realize that it was Jesse Belvin who taught me how to sing. Period.

Thank you, Jesse.

Enjoy the beautiful smooth voice of Jesse Belvin performing songs I have loved for all my life.

My grandmother's words were correct when it comes to Jesse Belvin: "Fifty thousand Frenchmen can't be wrong, honey."

By the way, the Gaynel Hodge, spoken of above, was one of the founding members of the Platters. He was a member long before Tony Williams and Zola Taylor joined the group.

***

Referenced Videos:

"Goodnight My Love"
https://bit.ly/2Xw13Nj

"Imagination"
https://bit.ly/3eDlGga

"The Very Thought of You"
https://bit.ly/2U5jhTD

"Angel Eyes"
https://bit.ly/3cqlZtj

"Making Whoopie"
https://bit.ly/2XUItxk

Chapter 17 – Johnny Adams and Curtis Clay

When you hear soul music or R&B or hip-hop or even jazz, it is generally produced by African American artists who grew up in cities, urban, as opposed to growing up in the rural areas.

They listened to music by their idols who were also from the city and whose music, despite the genre, was generally urban in style. They are people very much like me, who wouldn't know which end of a cow to milk if our lives depended on it.

But what about those who grew up in rural areas, maybe on farms, perhaps not, but whose musical idols were those they heard on the radio which played predominantly country music?

Some of these artists learned to blend soul music with country music and created a country soul musical genre. And the way they sing, it is truly incredible.

Today I present two of the absolute best in that genre of country soul.

The first is Johnny Adams, a prolific singer with an electrifying vocal range. One of the most remarkable voices ever.

The other is known for his stirring performances as a member of the Platters, but he is another powerful vocalist in the genre of country soul. His name is Curtis Clay. Curtis sings with a deep soulfulness that I know you will love.

Curtis and I are more like brothers than friends, and our friendship spans over thirty years now.

I remember that the first time I ever heard Curtis sing, I got goosebumps. I could not believe my ears. I think he will have that same effect on you.

These men are arguably two of the most excellent examples of country soul you will ever hear. Each approaches the genre differently, and both are inspiring.

***

Referenced Videos:

"Reconsider Me"
Johnny Adams
https://bit.ly/30fTz2P

"Please Release Me"
Johnny Adams
https://bit.ly/2U5jZ3f

"Blacktop Dreams"
Curtis Clay
https://bit.ly/36XIjcy

"Smells Like Rain"
Curtis Clay
https://bit.ly/2XQFTby

Chapter 18 – Frankie Lymon

The year was 1964. I was in sixth grade at Mill Elementary school in San Bernardino, California. The teacher had just finished writing something on the blackboard. She told the class to copy what she had written.

I walked up to the blackboard with my paper and pencil and started writing down the information. The teacher, sitting at her desk and reading something, suddenly looked up and asked me what I was doing standing at the blackboard instead of sitting in my seat. I told her I was copying what she had written, just as she had instructed us to do.

She asked why I was not doing that from my desk. I told her I could not see it from there. She asked, "You sit on the front row, and can't see the words on the blackboard?" She thought I was kidding when I answered, "No."

Even the kids sitting on the back row could see and copy the words.

I was sent to the school nurse immediately, and the nurse gave me an abbreviated eye test. She called my parents directly from her office.

A day or so after this, I was sitting in a store called White Front in San Bernardino. It was massive for its time, but a smaller version of what Walmart would be when it reached California 20 years later.

When the optometrist came out to greet my mother and me in his waiting area, he took one look at me and turned as white as a sheet. Visibly shaken, he felt compelled to explain his reaction.

"Please forgive me, but I'm a huge music fan, and you look exactly like one of my favorite performers did when he was your age. Have you ever heard of Frankie Lymon?"

It was the first time I had heard that name. But, as fate would have it, perhaps six months later, an article about Frankie Lymon came out in *Ebony* magazine, and it had pictures. When I saw what Frankie looked like, I could understand the optometrist's reaction. I did look very much like Frankie did when he was my age, and that puzzled me (and led me off onto one of my many tangents, this time researching doppelgangers).

As fascinated as I was by our resemblance, I was mesmerized when I started reading Frankie's story. It was incredibly entertaining, but also, devastatingly sad.

Frankie was a super talent. The first Michael Jackson. That is what I have always called Frankie. He could out-sing and out-dance most of the entertainers of his time. He was a poised and articulate speaker, had a quick wit, was funny, and displayed tremendous self-confidence. And all of this at only thirteen years old. Some said that had Frankie not died so young that he would have been the Sammy Davis Jr. of his generation. Others have said he would have been on the same level as Sinatra.

In these exceedingly rare videos, you will hear Frankie on his first hit record and see him on his first TV show as a member of the Teenagers group. Later it became Frankie Lymon and The Teenagers. Then, it was just Frankie Lymon. And all of that in just a year. In these videos, Frankie is between 13 and 15 years old.

In addition to three live video performances, you will see Frankie's very brief interview in Great Britain, when he was about to perform at the London Palladium. He was only 14 years old in this clip, but I am sure you will notice how poised and personable he was.

And the last video is a clip from the TV show, Mysteries and Scandals. It is a summary of what happened to Frankie, and why he was dead by age 25. This part is a bit sad, so if you do not want to check out that video, I understand, but it is a cautionary tale about what too much success can bring about when one is too young and ill-equipped to handle it.

Though tragically, his life ended so abruptly, no one can dispute his musical legacy. When a debate arose as to if Frankie deserved a star on the Hollywood Walk of Fame, artists as prominent as Madonna, Johnny Mathis, and Billie Joel rallied on behalf of the long-departed Frankie. He received a posthumous star in 1994, though he died in February of 1968.

No, I will not leave you hanging. To finish my story, once the optometrist gathered himself, he gave me an eye exam. Afterward, he asked my mother, "Who has been leading this boy to school all these years?" My mother thought he was making a joke. He was not. He handed my mother a pair of glasses and said, "Put these on, and they will make you see the way your son has seen all of his life." She put the glasses on and began to cry.

I had been a straight-A student up until I got my new glasses. Not being able to see, I had always focused intently on my schoolwork. But now? Now that I could see everything all around me, my focus on books took a nosedive. But I could tell you exactly how cute Lynette Cash was in her new braces, or maybe they were not new. Perhaps this was just the first time I could see them.

And I hope to see you for the next installment of *The Saturday Morning Song Chronicles.*

***

Referenced Videos:

"Why Do Fools
Fall in Love"
https://bit.ly/2yZMkkf

"Goody Goody"
https://bit.ly/2Mru6v6

"Mama Don't Allow It"
https://bit.ly/3cp0JUx

London Interview with
Frankie Lymon
and the Teenagers
https://bit.ly/2Y0akfD

Mysteries & Scandals
"Frankie Lymon – Part 2"
https://bit.ly/2MoOFYX

Chapter 19 – Johnny Ace

When it comes to Johnny Ace, I knew I had heard that name before, but I never knew his story.

A few weeks ago, when I composed *The Saturday Morning Song Chronicles* that featured Luther Vandross, I came across Johnny Ace and his music for the first time.

Not long after Johnny Ace began touring with Willie Mae "Big Mama" Thornton (the woman who sang "Hound Dog" before Elvis Presley "covered" it), Johnny Ace began having hit records. In the two years that followed, he had eight hits in a row. In December 1954, he was named the Most Programmed Artist of 1954, according to the results of a national poll of disc jockeys conducted by the U.S. trade weekly Cash Box.

I wondered why he was not more well known to me, as I am a naturally born kind of unofficial historian of music (it is just the way my mind has always worked). But I also wondered why millions of others did not seem to be aware of him either.

The answer was simple. Johnny's meteoric rise to the top of the music industry came crashing down in one terrible moment of bravado and carelessness.

This information is taken directly from a great website called History Collection:

Johnny Ace was performing at the City Auditorium in Houston, Texas. It was Christmas day and during a break with his bandmates, he began playing with his .22 caliber revolver. This was not uncommon for Johnny Ace as he often played with his gun and would shoot roadside signs while they were driving from place to place. The group was in a happy mood and Johnny Ace had even bought himself a new 1955 Oldsmobile just an hour earlier.

Johnny Ace was pointing the gun around the room, even at his girlfriend and another woman. He was told to be careful with it. Johnny Ace was cocky and laughed at the concern. He said that he knew which chamber was loaded and which was empty. He held the gun up to his head and said 'It's okay! Gun's not loaded...see?' Unfortunately, what the people saw was the bullet entering the side of his head and killing the young singer.

'Big Mama' Thornton then ran out of the room screaming that Johnny Ace had killed himself.

Even though it was widely reported that Johnny Ace died during a game of Russian Roulette his bandmates and others at the scene state that no one was playing Russian Roulette.

The funeral for Johnny Ace was held on January 2nd, 1955. An estimated 5,000 people attended the funeral and the singer was buried in his hometown of Memphis, Tennessee. After his death, people clamored for his music and "Pledging My Love" was released after his death on February 12th, 1955. All of his singles were then released as a full album called *The Johnny Ace Memorial Album*.

Numerous singers have written tributes and songs that tell the story of the famed R&B singer who killed himself on Christmas Day. – https://bit.ly/2zNxduI

What a shame. Like Frankie Lymon, Johnny Ace was another member of the 25 years old when they died club. There are too many cautionary phrases that come to mind even to begin sharing them with you now. Talent lost. Life squandered: and all so unnecessary.

***

Referenced Videos:

"Pledging My Love"
https://bit.ly/3eI66jp

Chapter 20 – Al Kavelin

Every time I write a new *Saturday Morning Song Chronicles,* I see connections that I never recognized before. Honestly, I have a new revelation every single Saturday a.m.

This week it hit me that novelty songs have played a big part in my life, and surprisingly, in my musical career.

The three songs I will talk about over the next few weeks are "Alley Oop," "Itsy Bitsy Teenie Weenie Yellow Polka Dot Bikini," and "The Monster Mash." These were all songs from the 60s, a time when novelty songs were all the rage. I was a little tyke, and these catchy songs made a big impression on me. But I had no idea how strongly they would impact my musical career to come.

First up, "Alley Oop," by the Hollywood Argyles. That is the first novelty song I ever remember hearing as a child. I would go around the house, singing it a lot. It caught my imagination.

Now, listen to how strange life can be.

Al Kavelin, a musical prodigy, spent his life in music, and he formed many record labels as well as Kavelin Music, a music publishing company. The Hollywood Argyles recorded "Alley Oop" on Lute Records, and it became a number one smash hit. Al Kavelin founded Lute Records, and it was also Kavelin Music that published "Alley Oop."

Two decades later, when I wrote my first four songs, we (my father and I) wanted them to have proper arrangements. We went to visit a man named Tom McIntosh, a professional musician, arranger, and film scorer. He wrote music for *The Learning Tree, Soul Soldier, Shaft's Big Score, Slither, A Hero Ain't Nothin' but a Sandwich,* and *The Legend of John Henry.* (*The Saturday Morning Song Chronicles* will feature Tom MacIntosh in a future installment.) We went to Tom's home in Los Angeles.

He was a humble, friendly man, and one would have no idea from his demeanor, that Tom was a towering giant in the music industry. That is until he told us what his price would be to arrange my four songs.

Back in a time when you could buy a brand-new penthouse condo for mortgage payments of $175 a month (and salaries were comparable), Tom's fee for song arranging was $1000 per song!

My father was cool. He never flinched. But, when those words left Tom's lips, for me, the room began to spin. I thought I might need oxygen. Tom laughed. He had anticipated my reaction, and he had a suggestion.

Tom said that he had a young friend who was an excellent arranger. He told us the young man had so much potential, that the great Andre Previn had become his mentor.

Tom further suggested that the young man would charge only around $200 to $300 per arrangement.

That was still a lot of money for back then (getting just one song arranged was the equivalent of one month's mortgage payment and a month's worth of food for a small family), but it was at least within reach.

The name of Tom's friend? Frank Kavelin, the son of Al Kavelin.

Like his father, Frank is indeed a genius, and he not only arranged my songs but also included the charts that I still have to this day. He, along with Johnny Otis, produced the recording sessions of those four songs at Johnny's studio in Los Angeles, California.

Frank was happy with how the songs came out, and he told us about his friend, Wayne Henderson, of the Crusaders. He said that Wayne had just started his own production company and that he was looking for material for his new acts.

Frank called Wayne, and together, they set a time for my father and me to visit with Wayne at his home. When we got there, Side Effect was waiting for us along with Wayne, and they all listened to my four songs. (Those songs, cut on acetate discs, wore out quickly. Viable for 10-20 plays; they were for demonstration purposes only. They were like wax records in appearance, but certainly not in durability. Using acetates was a frugal way of getting your music heard by potential users).

Wayne and Side Effect loved one song in particular, and there you go. I instantly became a published songwriter when that song, "Baby Love (Love You Baby)," appeared on the eponymous *Side Effect*, the group's first album for Fantasy Records.

So, in large part, because of the massive success of "Alley Oop" on Al Kavelin's Lute Records (now run by Frank), and because of the money that flew into the coffers of Kavelin Publishing due to the song's success, Frank Kavelin, the son of Al, was able to pursue his love of music. In turn, Frank helped me to achieve my dreams.

But the connection does not end there.

Two decades after all of this, I became a professional singer and soon became the new lead vocalist of the Platters. Today, thanks to the research I have done for *The Saturday Morning Song Chronicles*, I learned that "I Give You My Word," a song recorded by the Platters, was co-written by someone I had the pleasure of meeting decades ago. His name was Al Kavelin.

Now, tell me there is not more to life than meets the eye.

I have written hundreds of songs, but only one of them has been a novelty song. It is called "Milk Duds." Novelty songs are fun to write and sing.

Over the next two weeks here at *The Saturday Morning Song Chronicles*, I will share with you the interactions I had with Bobby "Boris" Pickett ("The Monster Mash") and Brian Hyland ("Itsy Bitsy Teenie Weenie Yellow Polka Dot Bikini"). See you then.

***

Referenced Videos:

"Alley Oop"
https://bit.ly/301rpby

Chapter 21 – Bobby "Boris" Pickett

The second novelty song that greatly impacted me was a song played every Halloween since I was a child. It is called "The Monster Mash," and it was written and performed by arguably the coolest man in pop music history, Bobby "Boris" Pickett.

This song I used to sing everywhere I went for a time.

In the 60s, there came a song called "Do the Mashed Potatoes" that spawned a dance with the same name, and the country went crazy with this new dance. So, a lot of songs alluded to mashed potatoes in one way or another.

"The Monster Mash" (mashed, as in potatoes) took it in a whole different direction. Monsters were dancing their version of the mashed potatoes.

There was no real "Monster Mash" dance, but it was super fun to imagine how Frankenstein and the Wolfman would get down to the current sounds of the day. Of course, monster movies were the craze of the 50s and 60s, so combining a love of monsters with the love of doing the mashed potatoes seems a logical progression.

I have always loved this song. Even growing up did not tarnish my appreciation of it. So, you can imagine what a great thrill it was for me to discover that on an upcoming tour of the Platters, Bobby "Boris" Pickett" was going to be one of the performers touring with us.

The following is a quote from the book, From Karaoke to the Platters in which I described that experience:

During the Golden Age of Music, the songs of The Platters reigned supreme. They had higher charting songs than most of the other groups of the day, and they had more hits than any other group of their time. This thought came to mind as we played a tour of Hawaii with several artists.

After a few performances, the promoters elevated us to top billing, and we began to close the show. But we were there with some excellent artists like The Drifters, and Brian Hyland, who had lots of giant hits themselves. But others had only one or two big hits. Within that group doing the tour with us was a great and unpretentious man named Bobby "Boris" Pickett, the guy who co-wrote and sang "The Monster Mash."

It is funny, but our minds continually give us preconceived ideas about a person's looks based on several different things. I had heard "The Monster Mash" for as long as I could remember, and with a song like that, and a name like his, I imagined Bobby as a short, stocky, dark-haired nerd type of nutty professor. When I met Bobby, I was surprised to see a tall, lean guy with a California tan, and one of the most relaxed personalities I have ever known in show business. I enjoyed spending time with him on that tour.

When Bobby came out to do his show, his hair would be disheveled, and he would wear a white lab coat with a trick tarantula on a string. The tarantula would periodically dash up to his shoulder from the pocket of his lab coat, and then quickly run back down into that pocket. And if I remember correctly, the lab coat had what I assumed was fake blood splattered on it. Bobby would also wear what appeared to be thick glasses to create his mad scientist's visual effect.

But again, Bobby was so cool! He would walk on stage, look at the audience, and after a long pause, he would say, in his Boris Karloff voice, "I will now perform a medley... of my hit." The audience would roar with laughter, and so would I. – Allen III, Paul "On the Road with the Platters," p. 109. From Karaoke to the Platters. Kindle Edition.

Here are a few technical facts on the artist and the song from *Wikipedia*:

Pickett co-wrote "Monster Mash" with Leonard Capizzi in May 1962. The song was a spoof on the dance crazes popular at the time, including the Twist and the Mashed Potato, which inspired the title.
The song featured Pickett's impersonations of veteran horror stars Boris Karloff and Bela Lugosi (the latter with the line "Whatever happened to my Transylvania Twist?"). It was passed on by every major record label, but after hearing the song, Gary S. Paxton agreed to produce and engineer it; among the musicians who played on it was pianist Leon Russell.
Issued on Paxton's Garpax Records, the single became a million-seller, reaching #1 on the *Billboard* Hot 100 chart for two weeks before Halloween in 1962. It was styled as being by "Bobby 'Boris' Pickett & the Crypt-Kicker 5". The track re-entered the U.S. charts twice, in August 1970, and again in May 1973, when it reached the #10 spot. In Britain it took until October 1973 for the tune to become popular, peaking at number three on the UK Singles Chart. For the second time, the record sold over one million copies. The tune remains a Halloween perennial on radio and on iTunes. – https://bit.ly/36UfYDQ

Bobby "Boris" Pickett died in 2007. That news greatly saddened me.

***

Referenced Videos:

"The Monster Mash"
https://bit.ly/2z2pnNi

Chapter 22 – Brian Hyland

"She wore an itsy bitsy teenie weenie yellow polka dot bikini." These lyrics are from one of the most played songs in music history. This novelty song about a shy girl wearing one of those new two-piece bathing suits had everyone singing along.

With most novelty songs that hit big, you rarely hear of that artist ever having another significant hit song. I was stunned to learn that Brian Hyland, the singer of this novelty song, had other massive hits.

I did not discover this until we were on tour together in Hawaii along with Bobby "Boris" Pickett of "Monster Mash" fame, and all the other artists.

Brian is a quiet man, gracious, and genuinely kind. One thing I loved when I met him was that his 15-year-old son was his drummer on that tour. I thought, *How cool is it that he involves his son this way?* I was more than impressed.

Brian taught me that those who perform novelty songs could be successful in other genres too.

Yes, spending even a brief time with Brian Hyland was a pleasure and an education.

Brian started recording in 1959 and is still performing today. He sang "Itsy Bitsy" when he was only 16 years old.

Enjoy Brian's songs, "Itsy Bitsy Teenie Weenie Yellow Polka Dot Bikini," "The Joker Went Wild," "Sealed with A Kiss," "Ginny Come Lately," and his cover version of the Curtis Mayfield and The Impressions song, "Gypsy Woman." "Gypsy Woman" was the second-largest hit of his career. In all, he had three gold records with "Itsy Bitsy," "Sealed with A Kiss," and "Gypsy Woman."

***

Referenced Videos:

"Itsy Bitsy Teenie Weenie
Yellow Polka Dot Bikini"
https://bit.ly/3dtx8Lf

"The Joker Went Wild"
https://bit.ly/3cui2DQ

"Sealed with A Kiss"
https://bit.ly/2zNJ6Rl

"Ginny Come Lately"
https://bit.ly/2Xunoec

"Gypsy Woman"
https://bit.ly/2AD1DQ1

Chapter 23 – Ricks and the Ravens

Some women will tell you that nothing is more exciting than listening to a man with a deep, resonating, bass voice, especially if he is singing to them. I have seen it with my own eyes. I have been in vocal groups with superlative bass singers, and I have seen how thousands of women react to them and their performances over the years. It is amazing.

Today, when we think of deep voices in music, probably the one that comes to mind as the quintessential bass singer would be Barry White. And before Barry, there was Isaac Hayes. In each case, solo artists, and that is pretty much how we see bass vocalists today. But it was not always that way.

Rock and roll and the doo-wop groups of the 1950s owed a debt to the groups of the 1940s. The groups of the 40s set the standard for the new forms of music of the 50s. One group of the 40s that was stellar in this regard was Jimmy Ricks and the Ravens. Jimmy Ricks and Warren Suttles founded the group.

Many things made this group unique; here are just a few. They were one, if not the very first of the vocal groups, to give themselves the name of a bird, and because of their astounding success, suddenly there were groups with names like the Orioles, the Cardinals, the Flamingos, the Larks and the Penguins (Earth Angel).

Another unique thing about the Ravens is that their leader, who sang baritone/bass, was the one that was featured. He led on most of their songs. And I must be honest with you. Listening to him now from his recordings in the 1940s, I believe that he may have been the best bass singer of all time in pop music. He did not have the very lowest bass voice, but Jimmy Ricks had extraordinary range and vocal techniques that were more akin to those of a tenor or alto singer. Vocal gymnastics are nearly unheard of for bass singers. They are striving to hit and hold those low notes. But this guy sang all over the place with his vocal runs. You would be hard-pressed to find a more vocally nimble bass singer.

What else was unique about this group? Jimmy Ricks and the Ravens had perhaps the best singers in every position of any group I have ever heard, bar none. Ricks was one of the best bass singers of all time, but each of the vocalists in that group was not just excellent; they were exceptional, extraordinary; completely world-class. Had this group begun ten years later, when rock & roll was coming into its own, they would be a household name now, much like the Platters, Coasters, Drifters, Temptations, and Chi-Lites. But they came and went just before the party got started. A shame for them, and a tremendous loss for all of us, because we never got to hear them live. They were magnificent.

Most of these rare recordings are probably songs you have never heard before, recorded in the 1940s and the early 50s. Back then, it was called race music before being dubbed Rhythm and Blues (R&B).

I was amazed to find that this group recorded "White Christmas" many years before my friend, Bill Pinkney and his Drifters recorded it with a great new arrangement and made it an international hit. But in the Drifters' version, you can hear that they based their hit tune on what the Ravens had done previously. Still, listen to how deep Jimmy Ricks sings it, and again, how amazing his technique was.

As you listen, notice the Ravens doing things that other groups who came after would emulate. For instance, hone in on the fact that each of the Ravens sang a lead part. The Temptations would come close fifteen or twenty years later, but even they did not have each member sing a lead regularly.

Notice how the high vocal, the soprano, would be preceded or followed by the bass vocal, much in the way the Dells would later do.

And remember that what you are about to hear had no multi-tracking. The guys had to stand there all together and sing at the same time. If there was a mistake by anyone, the whole song had to be re-sung from the top. Also, if someone was sharp or flat or their voice cracked, there was no pitch correction or way to re-sing that little part. Even still, you are about to hear some of the most beautiful vocals and prettiest songs ever.

I do not believe I have ever posted this many videos on one group before; however, each of these songs is so wonderfully written and performed with such beauty and grace that I had to include them. The up-tempo tune, which was their most significant hit, "Rock Me All Night Long," was my least favorite when compared to the other masterpieces they recorded.

As you listen to these videos, enjoy the stellar harmonies, the phenomenal leads, and the sheer beauty of the voices and songs of Jimmy Ricks and the Ravens. They are indeed gems in the history of modern music. Time has nearly erased them from memory. But I hope you will love what you hear and that from here on out, you will remember them. I know I will.

See you next week for a new installment of *The Saturday Morning Song Chronicles*.

***

Referenced Videos:

"My Sugar Is So Refined"
https://bit.ly/2XYDAmK

"Count Every Star"
https://bit.ly/3gPn6Gb

"Old Man River"
https://bit.ly/36UMYfr

"Please Believe Me"
https://bit.ly/36TEu8j

"White Christmas"
https://bit.ly/2U5EAoe

"You Foolish Thing"
https://bit.ly/2BmcSNc

"Who'll Be the Fool"
https://bit.ly/3dtyLZn

"Rock Me All Night Long"

https://bit.ly/3gMQPj3

Chapter 24 – Hazel Scott

You have, no doubt, heard of Billie Holiday and Ella Fitzgerald, but have you ever heard of Hazel Scott? Most of us have not, and the reasons for that are appalling.

Hazel was a pianist, a child prodigy.

To be admitted into The Julliard School (a private performing arts conservatory in New York City), is nearly impossible. To be accepted, you must be the crème de la crème, musically speaking. The age limit for admittance into this school is 16. But Hazel was so phenomenal that when she auditioned for the powers that be, Julliard made an exception, and Hazel Scott became their only 8-year-old student.

At just 19 years old, Hazel become the toast of New York and the world. Celebrities gathered at her expensive home to hang out with this extraordinary young woman. Her dear and personal friends included Duke Ellington, Langston Hughes, Frank Sinatra, Billy Holiday, Lena Horne, and Dizzy Gillespie.

Hazel became so popular that Hollywood sensed an opportunity, and they approached her. Hazel accepted, but there were conditions.

At a time when the only roles extended to female African American artists were those of portraying maids, servants, or prostitutes, Hazel Scott changed the game. She had it written into her contract that she would only appear as herself, Hazel Scott. Her demands included limousine service to and from the movie locations and final wardrobe approval for every role. She was so popular that Hollywood acquiesced, and Hazel went on to make five movies.

Before Oprah, there was Hazel Scott, the first African American woman to host her own regularly scheduled TV show.

As a recording artist, Hazel was world-renowned, and she refused to play for segregated audiences. If she got to a venue that previously claimed their audiences were not segregated and could see that they were, she would instantly turn around and leave the place, never to return.

Because Hazel fought the stereotypes that Hollywood continued to foster, and because she actively took a stand against the rampant racism of her day, she rubbed many who strode the halls of power the wrong way. Those influential individuals falsely branded her a Communist, a popular method for dealing with those who rebelled against the racial status quo of that time. America blackballed Hazel Scott.

So, the woman who was every bit as famous as her contemporaries Billie Holiday and Ella Fitzgerald dropped from sight in America, her name very nearly erased from the history of this country.

But Hazel was a force of nature and refused to let this unfair treatment stop her. She moved to France and took Europe by storm.

Hazel, a proud black woman who stood up for herself and all other black women, grew into the role of a fearless advocate of civil rights, and this was before Martin Luther King had come into full effect as a leader.

I have only one video for you today. It is entitled, "What Ever Became of Hazel Scott?" This clip showcases her immense musical talent and succinctly sheds light on one of the most gifted, powerful, and talented African American women to ever walk this planet. When you see her story, I trust you will be as inspired by her as I have been.

See you next week for another installment of *The Saturday Morning Song Chronicles*.

***

Referenced Videos:

What Ever Became of Hazel Scott?
https://bit.ly/3gJefG9

Chapter 25 – Tom McIntosh

The very first musician I met in my efforts to enter the world of music was Tom McIntosh. I had written four songs, and my father and I traveled to Los Angeles to meet with Tom to see if he would arrange those songs so that I could record them in a studio.

Back in the day, all songs needed written charts and studio musicians. There were no beat-making machines, loops, laptops, pitch correctors, sequencers, drum machines, and the like. Even synthesizers were brand new and considered avant-garde in music.

You wrote a song and took it to an arranger who created charts so that the bass player, pianist, guitar player, and drummer knew what to play, and they played what the arranger had written.

You hired background singers, who also had charts, so they had to know how to read music and vocally blend with the other background singers too. And then, you had your singer to perform, the engineer to record, the producer to produce, the mixing engineer to mix, and the mastering engineer to master the entire project and make it sound good in case it ever got played on the radio stations.

Whew! You can see why creating even a single 45 record back then ran a minimum of $10,000, a staggering amount when rent for a lovely home was less than $200 a month.

With a minimum of 10 songs per album, it cost at least $100,000 to produce a decent one. That is why there were precious few independent artists then. Only powerful record companies (and significant independent record labels like A&M Records and Motown Records with worldwide distribution usually provided by the big record companies through co-partnership deals), could afford all of this.

Producing an album was more expensive than purchasing an average house back then.

Anyway, we went to Tom in hopes that he would arrange our songs, the first step of creating our demo records. If we were going to attract the record companies, we needed professionally arranged songs.

But Tom's fee was $1,000 per song, and when he said that he almost needed to break out the smelling salts for me. That was two months' salary for me back then, and I do not mean net, that was gross salary! (And others were envious that I was making that much money back then. Lol).

It was Tom who recommended we contact Frank Kavelin, a great new arranger who would charge much less. (Frank's dad, Al Kavelin, was the founder of Lute Records. the label that recorded the mega-hit novelty song, "Alley Oop.")

Frank did indeed create arrangements for the four songs, and, after the recording sessions in the studio of Johnny Otis went so well, Frank put us directly in contact with Wayne Henderson of the Crusaders.

Wayne connected me with Augie Johnson and the other members of Side Effect, who recorded one of those songs on their first album with Fantasy Records.

And later, Wayne asked me to write the lyrics for "Always There."

Life is so exciting.

I knew that Tom McIntosh was a professional arranger and that he had done the soundtrack for a movie that achieved critical acclaim, called *The Learning Tree*. That is why we went to him in the first place. But I had no idea what a giant in the field of music Tom was. Here is a quote from a website called *DISCOGS*:

Tom McIntosh (born February 6, 1927, in Baltimore, Maryland, USA) is an American trombonist, composer, and arranger. He has worked with Dizzy Gillespie, James Moody, Milt Jackson, Duke Ellington, and Tommy Flanagan, among others. He was also one of the founding members of New York Jazz Sextet. – https://bit.ly/3gNKPGT

And, *Wikipedia* adds:

In 1969, McIntosh gave up jazz and moved to Los Angeles to pursue a career in film and television composing. He wrote music for *The Learning Tree, Soul Soldier, Shaft's Big Score, Slither, A Hero Ain't Nothin' but a Sandwich,* and *The Legend of John Henry.* In 2008, McIntosh was named a Jazz Master by the National Endowment for the Arts. McIntosh died in his sleep on July 26, 2017. – https://bit.ly/2Mmwqn7

So, we asked Tom to arrange the songs of a kid who was a meter reader for the Southern California Gas Company, when he had already arranged songs for Art Blakey, Illinois Jacquet, James Moody, and Milt Jackson.

Thank goodness, Tom was a kind man, and instead of laughing us out of the room, he connected us with a man who would help me begin my professional music career with a bang.

But here is another reason I will always be grateful to Tom McIntosh. He became a friend of the family, and he stopped by to visit us one time when my son, Paul IV, was about three years old.

I told Tom that when Paul IV was between one and two years old, that he would stand in his playpen and hold on to the netting and bounce in time to the rhythm of the music. He did this every time he heard music, and it did not matter how the tempo changed from song to song, Paul IV would bounce in perfect time to it.

Tom was fascinated, and he had me bring Paul IV to him. Then I watched as Tom tested Paul IV with musical rhythms. Tom could not believe what he was seeing. He told me to put Paul IV in piano lessons immediately.

My wife and I did that, and just a few months later, when I came home from work one day, my wife told me that as she was playing guitar earlier that day, Paul IV said to her, "Mommy, that G you just played wasn't right."

I got excited at what I knew this could mean, but I could not believe it was true. So, I put Paul IV in his bedroom down the hall, and I played different piano notes in the living room. I told Paul IV to let me know what notes I was playing. Each piano key I touched Paul IV would immediately call out the name of that key. "That's an A, Daddy. That's C. That's B flat, Daddy."

We knew that Paul's sense of rhythm was so accurate that it was uncanny. Now we learned that he also had perfect pitch.

Paul IV stayed in piano lessons until he was around 13 years old, and even now, he is still the one of the most gifted musician, singer, and songwriter I have ever known. Today he is the program director of 101.3 FM Mind and Soul Radio in Omaha, Nebraska.

He is also co-manager of a unique place called the Hi-Fi House in Omaha. The magnificent Kate Dussault founded it. There you can go and listen to vinyl records that date from the 1940s up to the latest releases of today: what a fantastic place. Kate is opening the Hi-Fi House in other states as we speak.

Thank you, Tom McIntosh, for what you did for me, my son, and our family. You, my brother, are deeply loved, tremendously appreciated, and sorely missed.

***

Referenced Videos:

"The Cupbearers"
Tom McIntosh
Benny Golson
James Moody
Jimmy Owens
Kenny Barron
Richard Davis
Stephon Harris
https://bit.ly/30a6Slj

Chapter 26 – Eartha Kitt

IMDb (*International Movie Database*) has what they call a mini-bio on Eartha Kitt that is informative and concise. It says of her:

An out-of-wedlock child, Eartha Kitt was born in the cotton fields of South Carolina. Kitt's mother was a sharecropper of African-American and Cherokee Native American descent. Her father's identity is unknown.

Given away by her mother, she arrived in Harlem at age nine. At 15, she quit high school to work in a Brooklyn factory. As a teenager, Kitt lived in friends' homes and in the subways. However, by the 1950s, she had sung and danced her way out of poverty and into the spotlight: performing with the Katherine Dunham Dance Troupe on a European tour, soloing at a Paris nightclub and becoming the toast of the Continent.

Orson Welles called her 'the most exciting girl in the world.' Eartha spoke out on hard issues.

She took over the role of Catwoman for the third and final season of the television series Batman (1966), replacing Julie Newmar.

Eartha Kitt died of colon cancer in her home in Weston, Connecticut, on Christmas Day 2008. –
https://imdb.to/3dwlmj3

That says a lot about this truly remarkable woman, but there is a lot that it does not say.

That biography does not tell us that her father was white and that she was more than likely the product of a rape.

Nor does it mention that her mother gave her away because her new husband, now step-father to Eartha, did not want a child of mixed race in his home. (Translation: Eartha received racist treatment from black people.)

And, that the relative who took her in when her mother gave her away may have been Eartha's actual birth-mother who had given her away first because she was ashamed.

Eartha spent her entire adult life trying to learn the identity of her white father and was frustrated at every turn by racism, which blocked her from finding out. (Translation: Eartha received racist treatment from white people).

Do you remember the biography saying that Eartha went to a new home when she was nine years old and that she was living with friends and in the subway as a teenager? Abused, Eartha felt she had no other choice.

Many who found themselves in Eartha's circumstances would have given up, but she was an extraordinary woman.

Instead of ending it all or choosing a self-destructive way of life, Eartha learned to speak Dutch, French, and German and became one of the most versatile entertainers of all time. She was a successful singer, actress, dancer, comedian, activist, author, and songwriter.

And when she had a child, she took her young daughter with her on the road (and pretty much everywhere else she went). She refused to allow her daughter to suffer the atrocities that she had experienced as a waif.

One last additional fact is that there was something quirky about Eartha's voice that mesmerized people and made them want to listen to her.

There is so much more to learn about this tiny but bigger-than-life personality that it would take an entire book to record it all. Maybe two.

You will find an excellent article about her referenced below if you would like to read more about this genuinely fascinating woman.

But this is *The Saturday Morning Song Chronicles*, emphasis on the word song, and Eartha sang two of them that I believe are absolute miracles of lyric writing. Each made me question my legitimacy as a songwriter.

These lyrics are witty, funny, intricate, evocative, and loaded with double entendre. Eartha's delivery is mesmerizing and flawless.

Enjoy "Santa Baby" (she was the first to ever sing the song, back in 1953) and "I Want to be Evil." I am presenting the videos of her performing these songs so that you can not only hear the brilliantly clever lyrics but so that you may also marvel at Eartha's delivery.

You will never forget her intense rendition of "I Want to be Evil" (which I found to be a little frightening, even though it is a funny song), and her sensual, suggestive, and coy delivery of "Santa Baby."

Another video features one of Eartha's biggest hits. Based on her voice and performance, this song gets my vote as perhaps the most sensual in pop music history. "C'est Si Bon," showcases how fluently Eartha spoke French and how seductive her voice and performances could be.

All three videos are historic gems.

Ladies, family, friends, and fans, please read about Eartha. Her journey was mind-blowing, and I guarantee that after you read about her in the article listed below, you will be inspired and feel even more empowered as your journey continues.

"Eartha Kitt" – *Wikipedia* – https://bit.ly/3dvVOT4

***

Referenced Videos:

"I Want to be Evil"
https://bit.ly/3cx5KdM

"Santa Baby"
https://bit.ly/3gOZXE0

"C'est Si Bon"
https://bit.ly/2XqDhC6

Chapter 27 – Peaches and Herb

One of the rarest types of groups in R&B, pop, and soul music is the duo, with a male and female lead vocalist. Don't get me wrong; there have been stars who teamed up to sing duets from time to time. There was Lionel Ritchie and Diana Ross. And who will ever forget the heaven-made match of Marvin Gaye and Tammi Terrell? Of course, one of my all-time favorite vocal match-ups was Donny Hathaway and Roberta Flack. And you must admit that it is pure fun to listen to Barbara Streisand and Barry Gibb, as well as Kenny Rodgers and Dolly Parton.

But a dedicated male/female duo is extremely rare. I loved Ashford and Simpson, Sonny and Cher, and then there was Peaches and Herb.

The great Van "The Hustle" McCoy brought Peaches and Herb together, and they made music history. Many know their hit songs, from the late 1970s, "Shake Your Groove Thing" and "Reunited" and one of the biggest "wedding songs" ever, "I Pledge My Love," but many do not know that this group had significant hits ten years earlier, and they were not doing songs like "Shake Your Groove Thing." They were doing some of the sweetest romantic ballads in music history. That was the Peaches and Herb with whom I fell in love.

Here is a brief bit of information about Peaches and Herb recorded at *Wikipedia*:

Peaches & Herb are an American vocalist duo. Herb Fame (born October 1, 1942) has remained a constant as "Herb" since the duo was created in 1966; seven different women have filled the role of "Peaches", most notably Francine "Peaches" Hurd Barker (April 28, 1947 – August 13, 2005), the original "Peaches" who lent her nickname to the duo, and Linda Greene, the third "Peaches", who appeared on the duo's biggest hits "Shake Your Groove Thing" (1978) and "Reunited" (1979)." – https://bit.ly/2MryY36

Here are their early hits, all from 1967, and where each song charted on *Billboard* magazine. You may not have associated these tunes with their later releases:

"Close Your Eyes" #8
"For Your Love" #20
"Two Little Kids" #31
"Let's Fall in Love" #21
"Love is Strange" #13
"United" #46
https://bit.ly/2MryY36

After all these hits, in the year 1970, for what is called in *Wikipedia*, "personal reasons," the duo disbanded, and Herb went into law enforcement, joining the Washington D.C. police department.

But I can tell you from experience that when music is in your blood, there is no getting away from it. Sometime later, Herb brought the group back together with a new "Peaches" and started performing again, releasing good songs, but no hits until the late '70s with "Peaches" number three.

Though they began way back in 1966, Peaches and Herb are still performing. I have that on good authority from a very dear friend. She is a fantastic entertainer, and she has been on recent tours where Peaches and Herb are one of the featured acts.

I also saw a recent video where Herb is still looking and sounding phenomenal with yet another "Peaches." I have always believed that Herb is one of the most underrated male vocalists in music.

If you are having pancakes this morning, get ready to douse them in some of the most sugary love ballads you have ever heard. As you watch these rare videos, notice the chemistry that Peaches and Herb have always had on stage, no matter which "Peaches" happened to be the latest in succession. Powerful stuff!

Thanks for joining me today, and I hope to see you here next week for another installment of *The Saturday Morning Song Chronicles.*

***

Referenced Videos:

"Close Your Eyes"
https://bit.ly/36YaHv9

"For Your Love"
https://bit.ly/2U9xUp4

"Two Little Kids"
https://bit.ly/2XTR0Ra

"Let's Fall In Love"
https://bit.ly/3eRya41

"Love Is Strange"
https://bit.ly/3dvnzLI

"(We'll Be) United"
https://bit.ly/2XW3jfx

"Shake Your Groove Thing"
https://bit.ly/3ePEFnB

"Reunited"
https://bit.ly/3ePEPvd

"I Pledge My Love To You"
https://bit.ly/3gQRzne

Chapter 28 – The Orlons

It was hard to classify the music of that time. This window extended from the mid-1950s to the early 1960s. Guys like Mitch Miller were having hit records and hosting musical television shows. Mitch was a musician, a record producer, and head of Artists and Repertoire (A&R – the guys who find and sign new talent to record companies) for Mercury Records and later for the juggernaut called Columbia Records (now called Sony).

I remember viewing Sing Along with Mitch before I was even in kindergarten. To get an idea of what was passing as the popular music (pop music) of the day, I present an abbreviated clip from one of Mitch's programs. The clip also contains the commercials that aired in the show, and they are fascinating in and of themselves. I hope you enjoy the video.

With songs like Mitch's version of "The Yellow Rose of Texas" being a hit on the radio, you get a good idea of the climate of pop music.

But at the same time, so-called "race" records (later called Rhythm and Blues, and then R&B) were enjoyed by black America, and secretly being purchased and enjoyed by the teenaged children of white America.

The Beatles had not yet made an impact on the music scene. At this time, the guys who would become the Beatles, and the guys who would become the *Rolling Stones*, were also listening to American race records in England and laying a foundation for what was to come in their music.

So, there was this mixture of genre and generations happening in music. On the one hand, you had the nearly sterile music of Mitch, who was appealing to the general white and adult masses. On the other hand, you had Rhythm and Blues songs like "Hound Dog" by Big Mama Thornton, playing underground, and being embraced by black people, young white teens, and white artists who would make this music their own. Some white artists determined to introduce their version of race music to mainstream white America and the world.

A prime example of this was Elvis Presley, whose later version of "Hound Dog" completely eclipsed that of Big Mama Thornton, whose listening audience was minuscule by comparison. Walk up to anyone in the world and sing, "You ain't nothin' but a hound dog," and they will say, "Elvis!" Precious few will say, "Big Mama Thornton."

So again, we are talking about the time between Mitch Miller, but before the time of the Beatles.

I'm sure you have heard of the Platters ("Only You," "The Great Pretender," and "Smoke Gets In Your Eyes," to name a few), and they were unique in that they had a female brought into the group of four guys.

Well, there is a group that took the opposite direction. It was a trio of female vocalists, and they added a guy to the group, and then they had some major pop hits. I remember running up and down our dead-end street, singing their songs as I played.

Here is what *Wikipedia* has to say about this three-woman, one-man group called the Orlons:

The quartet consisted of lead singer Rosetta Hightower (June 23, 1944 – August 2, 2014), Shirley Brickley (December 9, 1944 – October 13, 1977), Marlena Davis (October 4, 1944 – February 27, 1993) and Stephen Caldwell (born November 22, 1942).

Before they became The Orlons, they were an all-girl quintet called Audrey and the Teenettes. They formed in the late 1950s in junior high school and consisted of Hightower, Davis, and three Brickley sisters: Shirley, Jean, and Audrey. However, after the Brickleys' mother did not permit 13-year-old Audrey to sing in certain nightclubs with the group, she and Jean quit, making the group a trio.

In high school, the group's three remaining members discovered fellow student Stephen Caldwell, who was the lead singer of a local group called the Romeos. Impressed, they invited him to join the group in 1960 and named themselves The Orlons as a tongue-in-cheek nod to the friendly rivalry they had with a popular group at their high school, the Cashmeres. (Orlon was a brand name for the widely used synthetic fiber acrylic.)

A high school friend, Dovells lead singer Len Barry [My Note: Len had the hit song "1-2-3" on which the Funk Brothers of Motown secretly played], encouraged them to audition for Cameo-Parkway Records at the turn of the decade. The group took his advice in the fall of 1961, but were rejected at first, although the record label signed the group after two more auditions. Cameo executive Dave Appell appointed Hightower as the lead singer and began writing songs for them. – https://bit.ly/2Y0xqT4

This talented group sang the original background vocals for the mega-hits called, "Mash Potato Time" and "Give Me Gravy (For My Mashed Potatoes)" recorded initially by Dee-Dee Sharp. But when the Orlons recorded their first album as a group, they covered these songs by Dee-Dee and had hits with them too.

What were the other hit tunes of the Orlons? Again, this was a strange time in music, and I always looked at their songs as being just this side of novelty songs, but they still had enough R&B in them to make them super enjoyable and contagious.

Many of their tunes were about dance crazes of the day, like the Mashed Potatoes, and one of their original songs even started a new dance. It was the first time I had ever heard the word Watusi. Here is a list of their hits:

"Wah Watusi" (Tail wags dog and a dance is born)
"Mashed Potato Time"
"Gravy (For My Mashed Potatoes)"
"Mama Didn't Lie"
"Don't Hang Up"
"South Street"
"Not Me"
"Crossfire"

Do you remember these songs? If you do, I hope hearing them again brings a smile to your face. If not, I hope you will now enjoy and even be surprised by the songs of the Orlons.

The music recorded in that small window of time was something else.

Often in movies, they leave little hidden gems in the form of extra scenes that usually come in the closing credits of a film. The industry calls them Easter eggs. Here is my Easter egg for you this weekend.

My friend, Bobby "Boris" Pickett, had a hit called "The Monster Mash," and DJs all over the USA, and even around the world, still play it every Halloween. Listen to the background vocals of that song, and then listen to the background vocals of the Orlons as they sing "Mashed Potato Time" and "Gravy (For My Mashed Potatoes"). Bobby was paying tribute to the Orlons in his record, which came years later.

Have a great weekend, and I hope to see you again next week for another installment of *The Saturday Morning Song Chronicles*.

***

Referenced Videos:

"The Wah Watusi"
https://bit.ly/3027Dwq

"Mashed Potatoes Time" /
"Gravy (For My Mashed Potatoes)"
https://bit.ly/3dsnV5S

"Mama Didn't Lie"
https://bit.ly/2P94QuJ

"Don't Hang Up"
https://bit.ly/3dvoA6u

"South Street"

https://bit.ly/2ABJfHg

"Crossfire"
https://bit.ly/2zMustz

"Not Me"
https://bit.ly/2Y2T2P0

Sing Along with Mitch –
Mitch Miller
https://bit.ly/2Xv2dZj

"The Monster Mash"
Bobby "Boris" Pickett
https://bit.ly/2Y0o49W

Chapter 29 – One-Hit Wonders

A "One-Hit Wonder" is an artist who has had only one recording that placed within the Top 40 of what is considered an official "Pop Music" chart, like the one at *Billboard* magazine. There are others as well, like *Cashbox* magazine (now online instead of a printed version), but *Billboard* magazine reigns supreme as the granddaddy of them all when it comes to music and its charting.

So, you don't have to reach #1 to have a "hit record." Land in the Top 40, and you're good.

Many of us may discount or even feel bad for the "One-Hit Wonders" but that is entirely wrong thinking. To hit the Top 40 charts even once is to breathe rarified air. That one-time event can be life-changing, financially speaking.

Also, you can tour for the rest of your life with that "one-hit" as did my friend, Bobby "Boris" Pickett with his song, "The Monster Mash." On tour, Bobby would come out on stage, and in his "mad scientist" outfit, he would glare ominously at the audience for a moment, and then he would say, very slowly, "And now," he would slowly look around, "for a medley," more hesitation, "of my hit."

That always brought huge laughs from the audience, and from me—every time.

But you get the idea. One Top 40 hit creates a lifetime of opportunities. So, if you have ever looked down on a "One-Hit Wonder," don't. They are smiling all the way to the bank, holding royalty checks that will come six times a year, every year, for the rest of their lives. (That is if they wrote the song. Once or twice a year if they were the non-writing artist.)

I have been thinking about "One-Hit Wonders" since my awesome Cousin Sandra mentioned the subject in her comments on last week's *Saturday Morning Song Chronicles*. As I began to approach this subject, it hit me for the first time that my musical career has been strongly impacted by "One-Hit Wonders." Yet another revelation gifted me by *The Chronicles.*

For example, in my first band, Raw Sugar, started by my younger brothers, Corey and Milo (a sax player and a drummer respectively), whenever we found ourselves in trouble on a gig, we would call on the one song we knew would work every time. When people refused to dance and instead chose to glare at us like Bobby used to glare at them, I'd turn around and look at the fellas (Gary Miles, Victor DeLeon, Steve Gutierrez, Manuel Vasquez, Corey, and Milo Allen), and they knew that look meant we were going for it! And from wedding receptions to Native American Casinos, everybody would hit the dancefloor the minute the band started playing, and I would sing, "Hey—Do it now! Yeah, yeah!" Man, it was on and crackin'.

Thank you, Rob Parissi, for writing and performing "Play That Funky Music," one of the greatest hit songs of all time. It was Wild Cherry's only Top 40 song, and it went to number 1 on *Billboard's* Pop charts. It sold 2.5 million records in the USA alone!

Rob, if you are reading this, I wanted to let you know that you and your iconic song saved us and our gigs more times than I can count. I'll bet it had the same effect for other garage bands all over the world! Thank you!

Do you remember the song, "Forget Me Nots" by vocalist and pianist extraordinaire Patrice Rushen? "Forget Me Nots" received a Grammy Award nomination for Best Female R&B Vocal Performance. It was also later used in the movie Men in Black with Will Smith and Tommy Lee Jones. I loved the song, and I loved this artist.

The Total Experience was one of the hottest recording studios in Hollywood, and as luck would have it, as Ronnie Laws and I were walking out of it, this petite, gorgeous woman was walking in. She was looking down, but as we were about to pass each other, she looked up.

"Ronnie!" She blurted out in surprise. Ronnie looked at her. "Patrice!" They hugged each other and were all smiles. They appeared to be two old friends who had not seen each other in quite a while. Ronnie introduced me to Patrice, and I felt as if I were standing amid music royalty. This petite woman who looked as if she could not have weighed more than 90 pounds, soaking wet had suddenly become a two-ton heavyweight, musically speaking, because her song, "Forget Me Nots," was a Top 40 hit, going all the way to number 23. It became one of the most played songs ever. (Radio, TV, Movies, etc.)

Patrice shook my hand, smiled beautifully, and told me that she was happy to meet me. Then she turned back to Ronnie and forgot I was there. All I could do was smile. I had no idea how I happened to be here with a hot musical star who was blowing up everywhere, and on the radio, at any time of the day or night, you tuned in. I was still a kid at the time. *Buddy, you're a long way from San Bernardino*, I thought to myself.

A song by another "One-Hit Wonder" got me, my first manager, as a singer. And I didn't even get to sing the song!

There was an ad in a paper or on the radio. This management company was holding auditions at a recording studio. It was right when I decided I wanted to become a professional singer, so I went to the audition in hopes of getting a manager.

The auditions were in Moreno Valley, California, a half-hour drive from San Bernardino. (A half-hour drive doesn't seem like your destination would be very far away, but a half-hour on the freeways of California can take you 30-40 miles under the right traffic conditions. Under the wrong circumstances, you may only travel 3-4 blocks in that amount of time.)

As I recall, about fifty people showed up. The deal was that each singer was to bring a karaoke tape to back them up as they sang. Then, most karaoke cassette tapes would have on one side of the tape a demonstration version of the particular song with a professional vocalist singing that song. On the other side of the tape, you would have all the music but no lead vocal, so that you as the vocalist could sing the song with a beautiful (most of the time) arrangement. My tape didn't have a lead vocal side, only instrumental music on the front side, and that same music with additional background vocals on the flip-side.

The studio engineer, with the owner of the management company standing near, would cue up the tape, get you situated in the vocal isolation booth, and then he would start the song, and you would sing.

They were only going to choose one person to sign. I thought with all those people there, many who looked like stars already, that I never stood a chance.

About halfway through, it was my turn. I handed the engineer and manager the karaoke tape of a tune by Billy Vera and the Beaters, their only hit song called, "At This Moment."

I went into the vocal isolation booth, put on my headphones, and stood at the mic, waiting for the music to start. When it did, I began to sing. After ten or twenty seconds, the engineer and manager stopped the music and told me to wait for a moment. I watched from the booth (unable to hear them talking), as they examined the tape more closely. Then, they turned the tape over and inserted it into the machine. We tried it again.

I started singing. The engineer and the manager were looking at each other with strange expressions on their faces. They stopped the tape again. They kept looking at the tape and shaking their heads. They seemed extremely puzzled. They popped the tape back into the machine again, and I started singing once more.

After another twenty or thirty seconds, I could see them pointing at me and laughing. They stopped the tape and told me to come out of the vocal booth. I thought, *Man, you must have really screwed up. They let everybody else do their whole song, and they didn't even let you finish the first verse. And, they're laughing at you!*

When I came out, the manager took me aside and said, "All those delays were because when you started singing, we didn't realize it was you. We thought it was the side of the tape with the professional vocalist singing, so we flipped the tape and still heard the same voice. It was perfect each time. We finally realized that neither side of the tape had a vocal and that we were hearing you!" He was shaking his head and chuckling again. He continued, "That's it. No matter what, I'm signing you, but I have to be fair and let all these other people finish their audition, so will you wait, please?"

I left that night, knowing that the stars were beginning to align.

I have continued to love and to sing, "At This Moment" ever since. Billy Vera, wherever you are, thanks for helping me take my first step as a professional vocalist.

Finally, it wasn't until I started researching this article that I had a second revelation. I realized that I, as a songwriter, am also a "One-Hit Wonder," though it has happened twice. My songs, "Always There," by Incognito, and "Such A Good Feeling" by Brothers In Rhythm have both been "Top 40" hit records in America and Europe. "Such A Good Feeling" has been officially named one of the "Top 100 Greatest Dance Singles of All Time" by *Mixmag*, the iconic dance music magazine.

I, like the other artists mentioned here today, have had other songs on the charts, but none of them were Top 40 hits. I'll take it, just as happily as I believe the other "One-Hit Wonders" mentioned this morning would. We are proud to have our names and our music written indelibly into the annals of music history. We are ecstatic to stand on stage and say, "And now, for a medley of my hit."

Enjoy these historical videos and, if you have the time and inclination, tell us about some of your favorite "One-Hit Wonders."

Thank you. I so enjoy your being a part of *The Saturday Morning Song Chronicles*. I hope to see you back again next week.

***

Reference Videos:

"Play That Funky Music" – Wild Cherry
https://youtu.be/SFiv9M577a4

"Forget Me Nots" – Patrice Rushen
https://youtu.be/W2XhhuM9GZo

"At This Moment" – Billy Vera
https://youtu.be/LO01sRRLKkk

Chapter 30 – Northern Soul

I was introduced to Northern Soul a little over a year ago by a beloved friend who had the unique experience of enjoying the Northern Soul scene during her formative years. I was captivated by what I learned, heard, and saw.

But what is Northern Soul?

I do not believe in reinventing the wheel. So, here is a succinct definition of Northern Soul by *Wikipedia*:

Northern soul is a music and dance movement that emerged in Northern England and the English Midlands in the late 1960s… based on a particular style of black American soul music, especially from the mid-1960s, with a heavy beat and fast tempo (100 bpm and above)… The music style most associated with Northern Soul is the heavy, syncopated beat and fast tempo of mid-1960s Motown Records, which was usually combined with soulful vocals. These types of records, which suited the athletic dancing that was prevalent, became known on the scene as stompers. – https://bit.ly/3cAYMVr

Northern Soul embraced lesser-known songs and artists, but not just from Motown. They did not want songs that were significant hits. They loved hearing the undiscovered music, the B-sides, and the like.

One of those stompers mentioned above happened to be recorded by a friend of mine, Mr. Al Wilson. For some time, Al lived in San Bernardino, California, where I grew up. Though he had a number one hit song in the USA ("Show and Tell"), he was a hugely underrated vocalist in America. Still, he was tremendously appreciated by the Northern Soul folk, as attested to by the fact that he had the number four best single record in the Northern Soul movement's history with his song called "The Snake."

Enjoy the music and dancing you will see on these historic and rare videos featuring "The Snake" and some of the other top ten songs of all time in the Northern Soul Movement. Also included is the first "Chart Hit" of a song from a Northern Soul record label called Soul City Records. That hit was by "The Duke of Earl," "Rainbow 65" vocal star, Mr. Gene Chandler. The name of his Northern Soul classic hit is "Nothing Can Stop Me."

One other video that I have added is by a group on Motown called the Elgins. If anyone remembers the movie The Temptations, you may recall the group's audition for Motown, and they said their group name was the Elgins. The secretary/receptionist, who was portraying Martha Reeves in the movie, gave them a smirk and asked, "Like the watch?" They changed their name on the spot.

If Berry Gordy also had misgivings about the name initially, he changed his mind because he later christened one of his groups, the Elgins. Their Northern Soul hit song is called "Heaven in Your Arms." I added a video reference for this song because the Andantes are singing the background vocals, and they brought the fire for this track.

You may vaguely remember some of these songs when you hear them. I know I did. But again, most of these songs were not hits in America and so did not get much radio play. The story was different for the Northern Soul folks. These songs were the soundtracks of their lives.

***

Referenced Videos:

"The Snake"
Al Wilson
https://bit.ly/2yWvzpU

"Nothing Can Stop Me"
Gene Chandler
https://bit.ly/2Xr3Ffk

"Heaven Must Have Sent You"
The Elgins
https://bit.ly/2XwbtMV

"You Didn't Say A Word"
Yvonne Baker
https://bit.ly/3gLa4K1

"Out on the Floor"
Dobie Gray
https://bit.ly/3dw1k8e

"Long After Tonight
Is All Over"
Jimmy Radcliffe
https://bit.ly/303tTGn

Chapter 31 – TV Theme Songs

Memorable music comes to us from many sources, not just our radios or streaming platforms. A medium that engages our eyes, ears, and imaginations is television, and the theme songs of our favorite TV shows are still running through our minds decades after the TV shows have ended.

We do not give much thought to the fact that these TV theme songs are music (in most cases) and that they are money makers in and of themselves, but they are, they most certainly are.

Paul Anka was a teen heartthrob of the 1950s, as well as an excellent songwriter. Paul wrote and recorded million-selling hit songs. But his most financially profitable song ever was the one he wrote for *The Tonight Show Starring Johnny Carson*. Johnny's show ran for 30 seasons, nightly from 1962 through 1992, and that Paul Anka written tune was performed several times during each televised program. It introduced the show, ended the show, and was the bridge used to transition between each commercial break.

Paul estimated that this song was played about one and one half million times during those 30 years. He got paid each time it played. How much? He was paid $200,000 a year, every year, for 30 years. Now, being paid $200,000 a year in the 1960s was the same as being paid $1.7 million a year today. I don't know about you, but as soon as I finish *The Saturday Morning Song Chronicles*, I'm going to learn how to write TV theme songs.

Many of these theme songs had vocal lyrics that told us the premise of the show. "Come and listen to my story 'bout a man named Jed, a poor mountaineer, barely kept his family fed. And then one day he was shooting at some food and up through the ground came a bubbling crude. Oil, that is. Black gold. Texas tea..."

I may have missed a word or two, but that was only from my memory, the introduction to the show called *The Beverly Hillbillies* that aired when I was just a kid. (I must throw in here that I, and every other red-blooded male watching TV in those days, fell in love with "Elly May Clampett," played by Donna Douglas.

I have been star-struck only once in my life, and that is when I got to spend an evening with Donna years later at a performance of the Platters. Out of all the stars and musicians I have ever met, she is the only one I ever asked for an autograph, and she gave it warmly. We talked together privately for a long time, and frankly, I was in heaven! I framed that autograph and still treasure it to this day). But many of the TV show theme songs or introductions were instrumentals, and again, just hearing the instrumentals today, I know what shows they introduced in most cases. How about you?

Today, please allow The Saturday Morning Chronicles to take you back in time to when you were a kid, and if you will, I guarantee you that you will be smiling this morning.

We have something different for you today, video clips that cover a decade of TV theme songs, and I have one for the 1960s, the 1970s, the 1980s, and the 1990s. Pick your era and listen to those TV theme songs and see if you can name its show. I have been around for all those decades, and then some, so I listened to each one, and I could not stop smiling

Man! What a trip down memory lane. Of course, you can listen to all of them too if you like. Each one is wonderful.

These clips display pictures of the TV shows as well. Notice a young Clint Eastwood and others who would go on to become major stars.

The video section begins with "The Johnny Carson Theme Song" so that you can hear the music that brought Paul Anka nearly two million dollars per year, for thirty years. And here is another little-known fact. For Paul Anka's song to be used as the theme song for Carson, Anka had to make Carson a "co-writer" which meant that Carson was also making $1.7 million a year from that same tune! I'm telling you, TV theme songs, here I come!

Please have fun. I am betting that these TV theme songs will jog your memory as they did mine. Get ready to smile.

See you back here again next week for another installment of The Saturday Morning Song Chronicles.

***

Referenced Videos:

The Tonight Show
Starring Johnny Carson
https://bit.ly/2XVlLVR

Guess The 60s TV Show
Theme Song!
https://bit.ly/30b2gem

Guess The 70s TV Show
Theme Song!
https://bit.ly/2Xrc2HK

*Guess The 80s TV Show
Theme Song!*
https://bit.ly/2A0BGKi

*Guess The 90s TV Show
Theme Song!*
https://bit.ly/3gLue6u

Chapter 32 – Happy Music

Music is magic and has been with us from the beginning, with music being perhaps the first of the fine arts mentioned in the Bible's history of humankind.

Music affects our mood. How many of us listen to music as we go about cleaning our homes or washing our clothes? Do we play slow, sad songs while we work? Emphatically not! We play up-tempo music: pumping and uplifting. The next thing you know that mundane task is finished, and we are ready for what comes next.

Are you melancholy and want to stay that way? There is music for that. Do you have to fight a war? There is music for that too.

I have a dear friend, an artist, who knows specific keys of music that promote physical healing, and we have all had some emotional, spiritual, and yes, even sexual healing in our lives, courtesy of music—and Marvin Gaye.

By nature, I am a happy guy. If you see me, I am generally smiling. I have always manufactured my sunshine and marched to my drummer within, but when I want or need to feel even more positive and energetic, I know just the songs that make that happen for me. I share my stash with you today, hoping that they may have the same effect on you.

Me, a manager? The upper echelon of Color Tile, a chain of home improvement stores, had apparently lost their minds.

My new store was so far away from where I lived that it took me nearly four hours to get there and four hours to get back. I had to work seven days a week, and I had to open and close the store each day. The store hours were from 9 a.m. to 9 p.m., and I had to be there early enough to prepare for the store opening and stay after it was closed to do the books for the day. On my drive back every night, I needed to be super-charged. Thank God for Stevie Wonder and his song "Do I Do." Stevie, that incredible horn arrangement, and those funky guitar riffs fired me up and helped me get back home safe and sound each night. "Do I Do" is still happy music for me.

I had the honor of performing at the Yacht Club de Monaco, one of the most exclusive clubs in the world. I was a member of the Larry T-Byrd Gordon Band, and as you can imagine, the clientele befits the venue. We began to play a James Brown song, and all of a sudden, Prince Albert of Monaco took the stage with us and began to sing the lead to "I Feel Good." We were all blown away. Prince Albert was fantastic! And talk about fun? Everyone present could see Prince Albert's joy and excitement as he performed that song. No doubt, "I Feel Good" is happy music for the prince.

I remember as a kid, all of us (my sister, two brothers, my parents and I) eagerly sitting in front of the TV (there was only one in the house in those days, generally speaking) watching *The Ed Sullivan Show*. We were awaiting the performance of this new group called The Jackson Five. When they came out on stage with little Michael singing lead on "I Want You Back," we all went crazy. It has been one of my happy songs since that night of Sunday, December 14, 1969.

Instead of sharing the Ed Sullivan clip with you today, I have chosen to reference the group's performance on *The Andy Williams Show*. The professional demeanor and the delivery of The Jackson Five had markedly improved in the months between the two shows.

Fast forward several decades, and I have found other songs that make me happy and keep me pumped up too. "Uptown Funk" by Mark Ronson, featuring Bruno Mars, comes to mind, as well as the incomparable "Happy" by Pharrell.

Enjoy these videos, get swept up in the happy, and we will see you next week for another installment of *The Saturday Morning Song Chronicles*.

***

Referenced Videos:

"I Feel Good"
James Brown
https://bit.ly/2CZX5EA

"I Want You Back"
The Jackson Five
https://bit.ly/370wWAK

"Do I Do"
Stevie Wonder
https://bit.ly/2XSizKu

"Uptown Funk"
Mark Ronson
Bruno Mars
https://bit.ly/2Xspo6m

Chapter 33 – Augie Johnson / Side Effect

Do you know the name, Augie Johnson? Perhaps not. But chances are, you have heard his voice.

Have you ever listened to the music of Frank Sinatra, Michael Jackson, James Ingram, Dolly Parton, Ricky Nelson, or Kenny Rodgers?

How about the music of Keith Moon, Kenny Rankin, Esther Phillips, Nancy Wilson, Bill Withers, Chico Hamilton, Warren G, Boz Skaggs, or Quincy Jones?

Perhaps you are a fan of Barry Manilow, Taj Mahal, Billy Cobham, Country Joe McDonald, Rick Dees, or Morris Day?

Or maybe you prefer the music of The Brothers Johnson, Helen Baylor, Willie Bobo, Ronnie Laws, Wayne Henderson and the Next Crusade, Pleasure, or Hiroshima?

Have you ever heard of the group Side Effect?

If you have listened to these artists, you have also heard the voice of Augie Johnson.

Augie was one of the most prolific and sought-after background vocalist and background arrangers to grace a recording studio.

Do you remember the Boz Skaggs song, "Lowdown?" Who could ever forget "Ooh, Ooh, I wonder, wonder, wonder, wonder, who?" This gorgeous and harmonically complex vocal background hook helped make that song a hit. Augie wrote those background vocal parts and was a primary BG vocalist (background vocalist) performing on the song.

And the first solo hit (and solo gold record) for Michael Jackson? That song was "Don't Stop 'Till You Get Enough," and if you have ever heard that song, you also heard Augie singing backgrounds.

Augie was a great lead vocalist and an excellent songwriter; to me, he was a true friend and brother.

In a previous installment of *The Saturday Morning Song Chronicles*, I mentioned that under the direction of Johnny Otis and Frank Kavelin, I recorded the first four songs I ever wrote right there in Johnny's professional studio.

Well, one thing always leads to another. Frank (who was mentored by Andre Previn), and whose father, Al Kavelin, was responsible for putting out one of the most significant novelty records of the 50s called "Alley Oop," liked how our recording session turned out. As a result, Frank phoned a friend of his: Wayne Henderson of The Crusaders (one of the premier jazz ensembles in the world). He knew that Wayne was putting together his own production company, called At Home Productions and that he was signing groups and looking for new material. Frank told Wayne about me, and Wayne invited my father and me to his home.

When we arrived at the appointed time, we found we were not Wayne's only guests. Already sitting on the sofa were three very cool looking people. There was Louis Patton, a powerhouse singer with a gravelly voice reminiscent of a David Ruffin of the Temptations or Melvin Junior of the Dells. Sitting next to him was Greg Matta, whose vocal range is out of this world.

As if that were not enough, sitting next to them was the drop-dead gorgeous Sylvia Nabors, whose crystal clear and beautiful voice I have always loved.

But there was a fourth member of this group. He was standing. That was Augie Johnson, the highly charismatic and super-talented de facto leader of this group called Side Effect. Looking at the four of them, I knew they would soon be stars.

Augie Johnson was also a very decisive man, and his word was bond. Wayne played my four-song demo record for all to hear, and when the third song rolled around, Augie said immediately, "We'll do this one." That was it: end of discussion. My mouth dropped open. *This guy doesn't mess around*, I thought to myself. I also thought, *It just can't be this easy*. But a few months later, the song Augie heard and liked, "Baby Love (Love You Baby)," was on the album named *Side Effect*, the group's first album for Fantasy Records.

A lifetime of songwriting collaborations between Augie and I began. We wrote some beautiful songs together.

I shared the following personal story about Augie with Augie's daughter, Tishema, and she gave me her permission to share it with you.

We hear stories about musical artists all the time: the good, the bad, and the sensational. But this is a story about Augie's character.

At my first taste of success ("Baby Love, Love You Baby" and shortly after that, "Always There"), I quit my job and did nothing but writing music with Augie and Wayne.

Wayne hooked up both Augie and me with Martin Cohen, one of the most exceptional entertainment attorneys in Hollywood. Cohen represented Frank Zappa, the Crusaders, Tom Waits, and several other music heavyweights. At Wayne's behest, Martin Cohen took on a new client, a flea-weight with the last name of Allen. I knew I was lucky to be there.

Even a year after "Always There" became a hit, the songwriting royalties had not started coming in yet. I was going broke fast. That is what happens when you do not grasp the business end of the music business.

So, the time came when I had to return to a regular nine-to-five job. No matter my dreams, caring for my family came first.

I dropped off the map so far as music was concerned. I was frustrated and disappointed. Again, I had no one to blame but myself. Nobody led me to believe that I was going to be rich in a couple of months. No one encouraged me to quit my job before the payments started arriving. Had I studied the music business, I would have known that it takes some time for royalties to come in, especially the international payments.

The bottom line is that I did not connect with anyone in music for several years.

Finally, I caved in and decided to attend the NAMM show. (The National Association of Music Merchants is the most significant annually held music convention in the USA and one of the biggest in the world, second perhaps only to the MIDEM held in France.)

The Anaheim Convention Center in California hosts the annual show. Once there, out of the tens of thousands of people milling around, the first person I ran into was Augie Johnson.

Our reunion was warm and heartfelt. Augie invited me over to his home after the NAMM show. When I arrived, I saw that the latest female member of Side Effect, Miki Howard, was now Augie's "significant other." (Miki has sung more of my songs than any other female artist.) Augie and I sat on the sofa, eating chilled fruit and catching up. As I was about to leave, Augie said, "I have something for you." He left the room for only a moment and came back with several envelopes in his hand. He gave them to me. He said, "This is royalty money from the attorney's office. They didn't know how to get ahold of you. I told them that I knew I would see you one of these days, so they gave the checks to me to give to you when I saw you."

Some of those checks were years old, but Augie had hung onto them all that time. He knew where they were, and he retrieved them promptly. He wanted to make sure I received every penny of that money.

As much as I loved Augie already, that just shot my love for him over the moon. What a good, loyal, and trustworthy friend he was.

I thought that for the attorney to give Augie my checks, based solely on Augie's promise to get them to me, spoke volumes about the attorney's trust in Augie.

Decades later, Augie and I were in the middle of his latest CD, working on a great new song together when he suddenly died. I was devastated. Augie was my brother and songwriting partner since the time of our early 20s.

I miss my friend and brother more than words can say. I was blessed to have him in my life, and his daughter and I often reminisce about the great Augie Johnson.

If you navigate to my "Songs by Other Artists" pages on my website (pba3.com), sprinkled amongst others, you will find the songs Augie and I wrote as a team. All the Side Effect songs here are songs that Augie and I primarily wrote together, except for "Always There," which I co-wrote with Ronnie Laws and William Jeffrey, and "Baby Love (Love You Baby)," which I wrote solo.

However, if you look at the video references below, I am sharing three songs. The first song is "Always There," Side Effect's signature tune.

The second song I will always feel is the most beautiful of the songs Augie and I wrote together, and it features Augie doing the lead on this song called "Catch It Fore It Falls." His voice is so smooth that it is even calming to the ear.

"Baby Love (Love You Baby)," my first song performed by Side Effect is the third video.

Enjoy, as *The Saturday Morning Song Chronicles* salutes one of the best and most talented friends I have ever had in my life, Mr. Augie Johnson. Augie, you were a musical giant and human extraordinaire. I miss you, my brother.

***

Referenced Videos:

"Always There"
https://bit.ly/2U5Mjm2

"Catch It 'Fore It Falls"
https://bit.ly/3dvSQhF

"Baby Love (Love You Baby)"
https://bit.ly/3eM015m

Chapter 34 – Instrumentals (1950s - 1960s)

Though I have loved to sing since I was a child, I have also enjoyed listening to instrumentals. They make up an exceedingly small percentage of popular music now. But in the early days of radio, instrumentals were king. Groups like the Glen Miller Orchestra, Duke Ellington, Count Basie, and Bennie Goodman ruled the airwaves, and the airwaves controlled what music you got to hear.

But, as in all things, the only thing that will never change is that things are going to change.

From the late 1950s forward, many of the instrumentals that made it onto the radio and into pop culture were from television shows and movies. Indeed, the first instrumental I ever heard on the radio was the theme from the black and white TV show, Peter Gunn. I found a clip of the very first episode of this show, and in the closing credits, just as in the opening credits, the "Theme from Peter Gunn" is playing.

Enjoy this three-minute clip. It will show you how far television has come and how dynamic this theme song, by the great Henry Mancini, really was. Nominated 84 times at the Grammy awards, Mancini won a total of 31 Grammys. That is more than Quincy Jones, Beyoncé, or Jay-Z.

Another semi-instrumental I remember from my early days was "Bang Bang" by Joe Cuba. This song was my introduction to Afro-Cuban rhythms, and the first time I ever heard the word burrito. At that time, living in Omaha, Nebraska, I had no idea what a burrito was. But shortly afterward, when I turned ten years old, my family moved to California, and burritos became like manna from heaven. Even now, five decades later, when I taste a delicious burrito, I close my eyes, slowly shake my head, and in ecstasy exclaim, "Lord—have—mercy."

In the same vein as the music of Joe Cuba was the music of Mongo Santamaria, with his song "Watermelon Man."

Instrumentals in other genres would follow. I loved the relaxed groove of Booker T. & the M.G.'s hit, "Green Onions." This group was unusual in that it was one of the first racially integrated bands. And it was a Booker T, a black man, leading this group of musical virtuosos that included the legendary guitarist Steve Cropper. I imagine they had some tales to tell about the venues they played or were not allowed to play because they were an interracial group. They deserve their spot in musical history for more than just their excellent songs and musicianship.

Then came the Ramsey Lewis instrumental hits, "The In Crowd" and "Hang On Sloopy."

After the success of "The In Crowd," drummer "Red" Holt, and bass player Eldee Young left Ramsey's trio to form a group called Young-Holt Unlimited, and they quickly had an instrumental hit as well. It was called "Soulful Strut."

If the music to "Soulful Strut" sounds hauntingly familiar, there is a good reason for that. Do you remember a song recorded by Swing Out Sister called "Am I the Same Girl?" Well, it was recorded long after "Soulful Strut," but both songs came after the great Barbara Acklin sang the original song. It was not a big hit. Someone had the idea of stripping the vocals and turning the song into an instrumental. A piano lead took the place of the vocals, and the Young-Holt mega-hit, "Soulful Strut," was born. I have added their videos directly beneath the Young-Holt video so that you can compare them. Great music begets great music. Thank you to my dear friend, vocalist Larissa Larissa—leader of the Larissa Larissa band, and a background vocalist with the legendary Chi-Lites—for making sure I had the complete story.

An interesting side notes, when drummer "Red" Holt left the trio, he was replaced in Ramsey's band by a young drummer named Maurice White, who would go on to found Earth, Wind & Fire, and would later produce one of Ramsey's most critically acclaimed albums, *Maiden Voyage*.

Of course, I knew many jazz instrumental songs since I regularly listened to the massive collection of jazz LPs my father had amassed. So, I was happy when I heard Dave Brubeck's "Take Five" playing on the radio.

By the way, *LPs* are what the hip and the cool of that time called albums. L stood for long, and P stood for playing, ergo, long-playing records, which typically ran for approximately forty-five minutes, as opposed to *45s*, which is what the in-crowd called the small wax discs that held three-minute songs, the average length of a song in those days. (Forty-five is the number of revolutions per minute the record spins on the turntable).

As I put together *The Saturday Morning Song Chronicles* this week, it hit me how many instrumental songs have been hits. There is no way I could present them all to you in one offering, so let's call this article Part One.

Here are the artists featured in Part Two:

Tower of Power
The Average White Band
Ronnie Laws
The Edgar Winter Group
Herbie Hancock
Hugh Masekela
The Crusaders

Next week there will be more great music and some stories I hope you will find interesting. I know and have worked with some of these artists and will be able to share some personal insights into them and their hits songs.

I will be excited to see you here for the next installment of *The Saturday Morning Song Chronicles*.

***

Referenced Videos:

Peter Gunn (First Episode)
https://bit.ly/2AEOLZG

"Bang Bang"
Joe Cuba
https://bit.ly/30gxP6X

"Watermelon Man"
Mongo Santamaria

https://bit.ly/3788pK9

"Green Onions"
Booker T. &
the M.G.'s
https://bit.ly/3eE1avU

"The In-Crowd"
"Hang On Sloopy"
Ramsey Lewis
https://bit.ly/2zYPSDB

"Soulful Strut"
Young-Holt Unlimited
https://bit.ly/2MpsOAD

"Am I The Same Girl"
Swing Out Sister
https://bit.ly/3hHHGrE

"Am I The Same Girl"
Barbara Acklin
https://bit.ly/3gIRDp4

"Take Five"
Dave Brubeck
https://bit.ly/2AEQazq

Chapter 35 – Instrumentals (1968 - 1975)

As I step back in time to research, it shows that instrumental music with R&B flavor had a modern-day renaissance between 1968 and 1975. There were so many influential artists and songs that took the nation by storm that it is incredible. And, though I did not know it at the time, one instrumental was going to change my life forever.

In 1968, Hugh Masekela, an African trumpeter, had a number one instrumental hit in America with a song named "Grazing In the Grass." A year later, a group called Friends of Distinction would do a vocal version of that Masekela hit, and their version would go to number three on *Billboard's* charts.

At that time, I was too young and innocent to know that "grazing in the grass" was about the effects of smoking marijuana and encouraging everyone to partake. But I was running up and down the streets singing, "I can dig it, he can dig it, she can dig it, we can dig it, they can dig it, you can dig it, Oh, let's dig it. Can you dig it, baby?"

People must have been shaking their heads at what they perceived to be the youngest pot-head they had ever seen.

Isaac Hayes had many hits, but none as famous as his 1971 instrumental hit, "The Theme from Shaft." It went to number one on the music charts. In today's referenced videos, you will find a live television performance of this song, and it is one of the best I have ever seen produced from a television sound stage. The sonic quality was extraordinary.

1973 was an excellent year for instrumental music with hits by Barry White ("Love's Theme"), and The Edgar Winter Group ("Frankenstein"). Although Herbie Hancock's song "Chameleon" just missed the top 40 hit status by peaking at #42, it became a jazz standard, coved by several artists in decades to come.

Two of my favorite groups of all time both put out excellent instruments in 1974. The Average White Band hit number one with their song "Pick up the Pieces," and Tower of Power had an album cut that showed the world how great an instrumental could be. My musical younger brothers and I marveled at "Squibb Cakes" from the Tower of Power album, *Back to Oakland*.

And then came the fateful year of 1975. One of the most influential instrument hits of all time was Van McCoy's "The Hustle." It started the line dance craze called The Hustle. The dance took the nation by storm. (There was the Puerto Rican Hustle which came way before, but it was a two-person dance, not the line dance that even I learned how to do back in the day.)

And then in 1975 came an instrumental that would change my life forever. To explain the history of that song, writer Denis Poole shares this story of this song on a website called *Soul Tracks*:

When Ronnie Laws sat down with William Jeffrey to write the song ˜Always There" the chances were he was not looking beyond his 1975 debut release Pressure Sensitive on which the track can be found. The story behind how ˜Always There" went on to become a club classic and a genuine Smooth Soul Survivor is an interesting one that owes much to the acid jazz movement prevalent in the UK during the early nineties.

Ostensibly an instrumental in its original form "Always There" provided the platform for Laws' urgent sax but did contain a smattering of background vocals. These came courtesy of the band Side Effect, far more than a group of session singers, who were already forging a recording career of their own. When they went into the studio in 1976 to record what arguably proved to be their best-ever record, What You Need, they included ˜Always There" that, by then, had acquired vocals written by Paul Allen... ˜Always There" was now out there, a vocal pile driver, and it was only going to be a matter of time until someone else picked up on it. However, it wasn't until the early nineties when acid jazz innovators Incognito discovered the tune that things really started to happen. With a penchant that has developed through time for including a variety of guest singers, Incognito has continued to push the envelope of its own brand of jazz-tinged soul and their choice of Jocelyn Brown to handle vocals on ˜Always There" was nothing short of inspired. Brown's truly breathtaking urgency made the song completely her own and led to its inclusion on her own 1999 ˜Hits' album. Other notable covers in the acid jazz idiom include a version by Never Left that can be found on the 1994 release ˜US Dance Classics and another from Avenue Blue featuring Jeff Golub from their 1997 CD Nightlife. An interesting interpretation can be found by Rick Braun on the 2000 compilation 30 Years Of Montreux Jazz Festival' but most pleasing of all is perhaps Incognito's own reworking of the number on their current release Bees+Things+Flowers. Deconstructing the tune to its basic elements and allowing Jocelyn Brown to sing in unfamiliar falsetto tones they effortlessly turn this club classic into a thing of beauty. ˜Always There" is a true Smooth Soul Survivor and one which will undoubtedly continue to feature in the years to come. By Denis Poole –

Soul Tracks website - New Smooth Soul Survivor – "Always There." https://bit.ly/36XXpyT

Why did Wayne Henderson of The Crusaders, who was the co-producer of the album *Pressure Sensitive*, the Ronnie Laws' album that contained "Always There," call me and ask me to write lyrics for this song? It was because of a crazy, kamikaze move I made when I first met him.

I took one of his Crusaders' instrumentals that I loved and put lyrics to it. Please don't ask me why I did it. To this day, I have no clue. But something inside of me said, do it, so I did. I have since concluded that it was the presumptuousness of youth at work.

After Wayne acknowledged that he had received my new vocal version of the instrumental song he had written for the Crusaders, he said nothing: I heard crickets. I will never forget that phone call. I thought, *Well, there you go. You just took a promising career and flushed it down the toilet. This man is never going to want to work with you again. I am such a knucklehead! Only 23 years old and already washed up.*

But a couple of months later, when Wayne decided that he wanted a vocal version of "Always There," he called me, so in this case, the presumptuousness of youth paid off.

Now, looking back, I ask myself a chicken or the egg type question. Did Wayne remember that I was rather good at putting lyrics to music, so that when he decided he wanted to make a vocal version of "Always There" that I was the man he called? Or did my unexpectedly sending him lyrics to his instrumental give him the idea of making "Always There" into a vocal version?

At any rate, Wayne called me on a Wednesday night. I took Thursday to write the lyrics, and on Friday, I drove from San Bernardino, California, to Hollywood and directly placed the song in Wayne's hands. I drove back home and forgot about the whole thing, until around six months later when Wayne called and invited me to come to a studio in LA to hear my new song that had just been recorded by Side Effect. I had no clue what he was even talking about until I arrived to hear "Always There" kicking down the walls of the studio and Side Effect standing there, as proud and happy as they could be. They had done magnificently.

"Always There" is now a classic jazz instrumental. The *Pressure Sensitive* album went to #25 on the Soul charts, and every saxophonist in the world has attempted to play it at one time or another.

The vocal version of "Always There" / "Such a Good Feeling" (my lyrics placed over other music) went to #6 on *Billboard's* UK Pop charts and number one on their American Dance charts. It is now considered one of the top 50 dance singles in the history of dance music, according to the venerable *Mixmag* magazine, the premier publication on dance music. "Always There" and "Such A Good Feeling" are now on hundreds of compilation CDs.

In the videos below, enjoy the original instrumental version, and do not miss the vocal Incognito version with their remarkable performance in London to celebrate their 35th year in the music business.

Thanks for hanging out with me here today. Please enjoy these vintage videos (and the newer ones too).

I am hoping to see you next week for the latest installment of *The Saturday Morning Song Chronicles*.

***

Referenced Videos:

"Grazing in The Grass"
Hugh Masekela
https://bit.ly/3eIL7gn

"Grazing in The Grass"
Friends of Distinction
https://bit.ly/3jLCFAa

"The Theme from Shaft"
Isaac Hayes
https://bit.ly/371fQ5x

"Love's Theme"
Barry White &
Love Unlimited Orchestra
https://bit.ly/3cuWWFo

"Chameleon"
Herbie Hancock
https://bit.ly/3eOgR3u

"Frankenstein"
The Edgar Winter Group
https://bit.ly/39BVLnE

"Pick up the Pieces"
The Average White Band
https://bit.ly/3cxHsQS

"Squibb Cakes"
The Tower of Power

Horn Section
https://bit.ly/3eGRNve

"The Hustle"
Van McCoy
https://bit.ly/2Mr9gMd

"Always There"
Ronnie Laws
featuring Tom Browne
https://bit.ly/2U7qYZn

"Always There"
Side Effect
https://bit.ly/3gLIbS5

"Always There"
Incognito
"Live in London"
https://bit.ly/2MnzcIE

Chapter 36 – Berry Gordy and Motown

I had a completely different article to present to you in *The Saturday Morning Song Chronicles* today, but earlier this morning, something changed. I read something that made me put the other piece on hold, in favor of bringing this one to you today.

Berry Gordy has announced that he is retiring from Motown.

I thought about that for a moment and about the impact this man has had on all our lives, and I realized that mentioning his legacy would be the most appropriate thing we could do this weekend.

Berry Gordy gave the world a tremendous gift that transcends color, class, national borders, language, hatred, and hopelessness. To us, he gave music that nearly everyone, everywhere, loved. Who would even want to imagine our world without Stevie Wonder, Smokey Robinson, Marvin Gaye, The Temptations, The Supremes, Gladys Knight, or any of the rest of the Motown stable of artists, engineers, songwriters, producers, musicians, and background singers?

This music is the soundtrack of our very lives, and none of us would have been the same had there been no Motown and no Berry Gordy. Job well done, Mr. Gordy. You are loved and appreciated beyond all comprehension. Thank you for the gift you have given us.

In closing, I would like to leave you with a few of my favorite Motown songs presented in historical and rarely seen videos. For a truly magnificent and powerhouse performance, whatever you do, do not miss the Gladys Knight video. I saved the best for last. She is truly the Empress of Soul.

If you would like to share some of your favorite Motown songs that have impacted your life, we would love to hear from you.

Enjoy, and I hope that you will join us next weekend for *The Saturday Morning Song Chronicles*, which will reveal yet another secret ingredient that Motown used to establish its incredible music dynasty.

***

Referenced Videos:

"My Girl"
The Temptations
https://bit.ly/3cthrSP

"As"
Stevie Wonder
https://bit.ly/2yYZ8qW

"Ooh, Baby, Baby"
Smokey Robinson and
the Miracles
https://bit.ly/3067Pee

"Don't Mess with Bill"
The Marvelettes
https://bit.ly/2Mra57L

"I Heard It Through
the Grapevine"
Marvin Gaye
https://bit.ly/2Ua98oO

"Neither One of Us"
Gladys Knight
https://bit.ly/30WHDS4

Chapter 37 – Marvin Gaye "The Prince of Motown"

Lou Gehrig of the New York Yankees had a nickname. They called him "The Iron Horse." Why? According to the website, *GermanHeritage.com*, "Gehrig was known as the Iron Horse because he established a record for the number of consecutive games played by a professional baseball player, appearing in 2130 consecutive games from 1925 to 1939." – "LOU GEHRIG: 'The Iron Horse'" by Shelly McDonald. https://bit.ly/3crRmUc

Yes, it was because of his consistency that Gehrig was called the Iron Horse. And his record stood for over fifty years.

If I had a "fantasy" musical team, Marvin Gaye would be my Iron Horse.

From his first record in 1962 to his last in 1982, Marvin Gaye had 67 singles that reached the *Billboard* charts. Just over 40 of those records achieved Top 40 hit status, 18 graced the Top 10, and 3 of his songs made it to number 1.

But here is the kicker. My mouth dropped open when I began compiling those singles and started plugging in the dates those recordings were released. As I was typing, I thought, *Oh, my God! I had no idea!*

Look at how many hit records he had per year. There were a few years when Marvin had only one or two (and any artist on the planet would be ecstatic to have even one hit record in their entire career), but there were years in which Marvin Gaye had three, four, five, even six hit records within the same 12 months.

And look at the years themselves. From 1962 Marvin had hit records every year until 1975 when he was touring so extensively that he could not get back into the studio. This list made me reflect on the greatness of Marvin Gaye.

I remembered my grandmother being overwhelmingly infatuated with Marvin, and I recall her playing his songs. I mean, she was in love! I was a little kid at that time, and even I could see that.

But then I remembered that Marvin had hits when I was a young man. And he had hits when I was married, and when my son was born, and he was still producing hits ten years later, not long before my daughter was born.

Marvin had hits as a solo act and hits doing duets with various Motown female artists, including Diana Ross, Mary Wells, Kim Weston, and Tammi Terrell.

Marvin Gaye was a hit-making machine. He was so low-key that I never realized he was pumping out so many hit songs! He was like a deadly silent assassin who let his music speak for itself.

Check out this list of hits songs he put out, and as you read these song titles, it will start to come back to you. I can hear you now. "Oh, yeah, I remember this song. Wait, I remember this one too." Like me, you will realize that Marvin Gaye has always been there through the events of our lives until the day he was no more.

Remembering that the definition of a hit record is a song that places in the Top 40 on the Pop Charts, here are the hit songs of Marvin Gaye:

1962 – "Hitchhike" #30

1963 – "Pride and Joy" #10

1963 – "Can I Get a Witness" #22

1964 – "You're a Wonderful One" #15

1964 – "Once Upon A Time" (Duet with Mary Wells) #19

1964 – "What's the Matter With You Baby" (Duet with Mary Wells) #17

1964 – "Try It Baby" #15

1964 – "Baby, Don't You Do It" #27

1964 – "How Sweet It Is To Be Loved By You" #6

1965 – "I'll Be Doggone #8

1965 – "Pretty Little Baby" #25

1965 – "Ain't That Peculiar #8

1966 – "One More Heartache" #29

1966 – "It Takes Two" (with Kim Weston) #14

1967 – "Ain't No Mountain High Enough" (with Tammi Terrell) #19

1967 – "Your Unchanging Love" #33

1967 – "Your Precious Love" (with Tammi Terrell) #5

1967 – "You" #34

1967 – "If I Could Build My Whole World Around You" (with Tammi Terrell) #10

1968 – "Ain't Nothing Like The Real Thing" (with Tammi Terrell) #8

1968 – "You're All I Need To Get By" (with Tammi Terrell) #7

1968 – "Chained" #32

1968 – "Keep On Lovin Me Honey" (with Tammi Terrell) #24

1968 – "I Heard It Through The Grapevine" #1 Pop, Soul,

1969 – "Good Loving Ain't Easy To Come By" (with Tammi Terrell) #30

1969 – "Too Busy Thinking About My Baby" #4

1969 – "That's The Way Love Is" #7

1970 – "The End of Our Road" #40

1971 – "What's Going On" #2

1971 – "Mercy, Mercy, Me" #4

1971 – "Inner City Blues (Make Me Wanna Holler)" #9

1972 – "Trouble Man" #7

1973 – "Let's Get It On" #1

1973 – "You're A Special Part of Me" (with Diana Ross) #12

1973 – "Come Get To This" #21

1974 – "My Mistake (Was To Love You)" (with Diana Ross) #19

1974 – "Distant Lover" #28

1976 – "I Want You" #15

1977 – "Got To Give It Up" (Part 1) #1

1982 – "Sexual Healing" #3

Please remember, these are only the bonafide hits. There were several other charted recordings as well.

Here are a few more interesting facts about Marvin Gaye:

Marvin Gaye added the "e" to his name to stop being teased about his sexuality, and to distance himself from his father.

Marvin, like Maurice White, the founder of Earth, Wind & Fire, was a professional drummer before becoming a famous vocalist. In our next installment of *The Saturday Morning Song Chronicles*, you will see what an excellent drummer he was.

Marvin penned most of his big hits, but he also wrote or co-wrote songs that other artists performed. Some of my favorites were:

The Marvelettes' song, "Beachwood 45789"
The Originals' "Baby, I'm For Real"
The Originals' "The Bells"
Martha Reeves and the Vandellas' "Dancing in the Streets"

Being inducted into the Songwriters' Hall of Fame or the Rock and Roll Hall of Fame is an incredible achievement. Marvin Gaye was a member of both.

And here is another fascinating thing about Marvin. When he signed with Tamla Records (incorporated as Motown Records in 1960), he pursued a career as a performer of jazz music and standards, having no desire to become an R&B performer.

Later known as The Prince of Soul, Marvin did not desire to sing soul music initially. How crazy is that? I found one of his old songs that demonstrates the kind of songs he wished to sing, but that Motown did not let him sing very often.

This song is from 1964. Keep in mind that most of his great duets and his songs like "I Heard it Through the Grapevine" would come many years later.

I hope you enjoy the video that showcases the beautiful voice of Marvin Gaye as he performs "If My Heart Could Sing."

Before we knew Marvin Gaye as a solo artist, he was a member of the group, Harvey and the New Moonglows. Marvin had his first-ever recorded lead vocal with that group on a song named "Mama Loocie." Enjoy these rare video clips that will demonstrate how much Marvin grew as a singer over time.

Marvin Gaye died on April 1, 1984, one day before his birthday. He was forty-four years old. He spent nearly half his life putting out hit recordings.

Marvin Gaye, "The Prince of Motown," was also the "Iron Horse" of music.

Thanks for joining us today. We hope to see you again next week for another installment of *The Saturday Morning Song Chronicles.*

***

Referenced Videos:

"Mama Loocie"
The Moonglows
https://bit.ly/2XxTyoM

"If My Heart Could Sing"
https://bit.ly/2A03yOP

"I Heard It Through
the Grapevine"
Marvin Gaye
Gladys Knight
https://bit.ly/2EoVl8C

"The American
National Anthem"

Marvin Gaye
https://bit.ly/3gOmfFX

"Sexual Healing"
Marvin Gaye
https://bit.ly/3gT9CJC

"What's Going On"
Marvin Gaye
https://bit.ly/307KBEo

"Let's Get It On"
Marvin Gaye
https://bit.ly/3gRQgEK

"I Want You"
Marvin Gaye
https://bit.ly/3cw4HLj

Chapter 38 – The Funk Brothers – Part One

Motown's music swept the globe and produced the hit records that became the soundtrack to the lives of millions of music lovers everywhere. Much of that great music is still around and being covered by various artists today.

There were many components to the Motown Sound, and one of the major ones was the stellar group of musicians used by Motown on their recordings. They came to be known as the Funk Brothers, and they were responsible for more hits than any Motown artist because they played on nearly every Motown hit from 1959-1972.

Standing in the Shadows of Motown, a video about the Funk Brothers says that they have played on more number one hits than the Beatles, Elvis Presley, the Rolling Stones, and the Beach Boys combined.

According to *Wikipedia*, the venerable National Academy of Recording Arts and Sciences recognizes 13 musicians as official Funk Brothers. Still, the name is often casually used as a catch-all designation to cover any musician who played on a Motown record.

The 13 recognized members are:

Keyboardists: Joe Hunter (bandleader, 1959-1964)* Earl Van Dyke (bandleader, 1964-1972)* Richard "Popcorn" Wylie (1959-1962) and Johnny Griffith (1963-1972)*

Guitarists: Robert White (1959-1972)* Eddie "Chank" Willis (1959-1972)* and Joe Messina (1959-1972)* Bassists: James Jamerson (1959-1972)* and Bob Babbitt (1967-1972)* Drummers: William "Benny" Benjamin (1959-1969)* Richard "Pistol" Allen (1959-1972)* Marvin Gaye (1961-1962) and Uriel Jones (1963-1972)* Percussionists: Jack Ashford (1959-1972, tambourine)* and Eddie "Bongo" Brown (1959-1972).
https://bit.ly/3cw1mvQ

You may have noticed I said there were 13 musicians recognized, but I listed 14 names. I got a kick out of the fact that some guy named Marvin Gaye was a drummer in the band from 1961-1962. Short tenure. Gee, I wonder whatever happened to that guy?

Here is a partial list compiled by *Wikipedia* of the hit songs on which the Funk Brothers were the musicians:

"Please Mr. Postman" – The Marvelettes * "Fingertips Pt. 2" – Stevie Wonder * "The Girl's Alright with Me" - The Temptations * "My Guy" – Mary Wells * "Come and Get These Memories" - Martha and the Vandellas * "Where Did Our Love Go" – The Supremes * "Baby I Need Your Loving" - The Four Tops * "Baby Love" – The Supremes * "Come See About Me" – The Supremes * "My Girl" – The Temptations * "Stop! In the Name of Love" – The Supremes * "Back in My Arms Again" – The Supremes * "I Can't Help Myself (Sugar Pie Honey Bunch)" – The Four Tops * "I Hear a Symphony" – The Supremes * "Love Is Like an Itching in My Heart" - The Supremes * "You Can't Hurry Love" – The Supremes *
"Reach Out I'll Be There" – The Four Tops * "You Keep Me Hangin' On" – The Supremes *

"Forever Came Today" – The Supremes * "Love Child" – Diana Ross and the Supremes * "I Heard It Through the Grapevine" – Marvin Gaye * "I Can't Get Next to You" – The Temptations * "Someday We'll Be Together" – Diana Ross and the Supremes * "Ain't No Mountain High Enough" – Diana Ross * "The Tears of a Clown" – Smokey Robinson and the Miracles * "Just My Imagination (Running Away with Me)" – The Temptations * "Papa Was a Rollin' Stone" – The Temptations * "Let's Get It On" – Marvin Gaye * "You Sure Love to Ball" - Marvin Gaye * "Come Get to This" - Marvin Gaye * "Just a Little Misunderstanding" – The Contours * "Shop Around" – The Miracles * "Shotgun" – Junior Walker & the All Stars * "How Sweet It Is (To Be Loved by You)" – Marvin Gaye * "The One Who Really Loves You" – Mary Wells * "The Way You Do the Things You Do" – The Temptations * "Ain't Nothing Like the Real Thing" – Marvin Gaye and Tammi Terrell * "(I'm a) Road Runner" – Junior Walker & the All Stars * "Ain't Too Proud to Beg" – The Temptations * "I Wish It Would Rain" – The Temptations

That was a big list of songs, wasn't it? Well, there are a few more:

"Reflections" – Diana Ross & the Supremes * "That's the Way Love Is" - Marvin Gaye * "Heat Wave" – Martha & the Vandellas * "Hitch Hike" – Marvin Gaye * "Who's Lovin' You" - The Jackson 5 * "What's So About Goodbye" – The Miracles * "I Was Made to Love Her" – Stevie Wonder * "It's the Same Old Song" – The Four Tops * "You've Really Got a Hold on Me" – The Miracles * "Standing in the Shadows of Love" – The Four Tops * "If I Were Your Woman" – Gladys Knight & the Pips *

"I'm Livin' in Shame - The Supremes * "Going to a Go-Go" – The Miracles * "Heaven Must Have Sent You" – The Elgins * "Dancing in the Street" – Martha & the Vandellas * "Runaway Child, Running Wild" - The Temptations * "Mercy Mercy Me (The Ecology)" – Marvin Gaye * "Inner City Blues (Make Me Wanna Holler)" - Marvin Gaye * "Cloud Nine" – The Temptations * "What's Goin' On" – Marvin Gaye * "Do You Love Me" – The Contours * "Get Ready" – The Temptations * "Function at the Junction" – Shorty Long * "My World Is Empty Without You" – The Supremes * "The Tracks of My Tears" – The Miracles * "Can I Get a Witness" – Marvin Gaye * "Nowhere to Run" – Martha & the Vandellas * "Here Comes the Judge" – Shorty Long * "Signed, Sealed, Delivered (I'm Yours)" – Stevie Wonder * "Beachwood 4-5789" – The Marvelettes * "Bernadette" – The Four Tops * "Two Lovers" – Mary Wells * "What Becomes of the Brokenhearted" – Jimmy Ruffin * "My Cherie Amour" – Stevie Wonder * "I Second That Emotion" – Smokey Robinson & the Miracles * "(I Know) I'm Losing You" – The Temptations * "First I Look at the Purse" – The Contours * "Ooo Baby Baby" – The Miracles * "25 Miles" – Edwin Starr * "I'll Be Doggone" – Marvin Gaye * "Pride and Joy" – Marvin Gaye * "Ball of Confusion (That's What the World Is Today)" – The Temptations * "It Takes Two" – Marvin Gaye & Kim Weston * "This Old Heart of Mine (Is Weak for You)" – The Isley Brothers * "Uptight" – Stevie Wonder * "Devil with a Blue Dress On" – Shorty Long * "Jimmy Mack" – Martha & the Vandellas * "Since I Lost My Baby" – The Temptations * "War" – Edwin Starr * "Stubborn Kind of Fellow" – Marvin Gaye * "Don't Mess with Bill" – The Marvelettes * "You Beat Me to the Punch" – Mary Wells * "Shake Me, Wake Me (When It's Over)" – The Four Tops

"Walk Away Renee" – The Four Tops * "Mickey's Monkey" – The Miracles * "Ain't That Peculiar" – Marvin Gaye * "Shoo-Be-Doo-Be-Doo-Da-Day" – Stevie Wonder - https://bit.ly/3cw1mvQ

I'll bet you have heard one or two of these songs before, haven't you? Who knew that the same musicians played on all these records, and thousands more?

If you would like to learn more about the Funk Brothers and their incredible story, there is an excellent musical documentary called *Standing in The Shadows of Motown*. You can find a seven-minute video clip taken from this documentary still featured on YouTube. I have provided the link.

As impressive as the list of songs above is, there is another list equally as impressive and considerably more shocking that I will share with you in "The Funk Brothers - Part Two." I'll see you next week for the latest installment of *The Saturday Morning Song Chronicles*.

***

Referenced Videos:

Standing in the Shadows of Motown
https://bit.ly/36WEsMW

Chapter 39 – The Funk Brothers – Part Two

Baby-boomer. Gen-X. Millennial. Until my dying day, I will proclaim that I am a Motown Baby. I do not think it is an official classification, but a Motown Baby is what I am. It describes me to a tee. And yet, other music moved me too.

When my immediate family (father, mother, sister, brothers), and I moved from Omaha, Nebraska, to San Bernardino, California, our grandparents missed us a lot, just as we missed them. They demonstrated that in many ways, but one tangible way was that from time to time, we would receive a large box of the latest records from A&A Record Shop. My grandparents owned A&A, located just across the street from the venerable Allen's Showcase nightclub, which they also owned.

And even though most of the records were not from Motown or Tamla (later incorporated as Motown), wow, did I ever find some treasures in those little musical care packages from "Grandpa Pop and The Queen."

There was the fun and bravado of "Cool Jerk," a song by the Capitols on Karen Records. "This cat they talkin' about, I wonder who could it be? Cause I know, I'm the heaviest cat, the heaviest cat you ever did see." Yes, he was indeed, "the King of the Cool Jerk!"

And then there was the classic song, "Rescue Me," by Fontella Bass. This song, recorded on the Chess label, was one I have always loved.

"Rescue me. Take me in your arms. Rescue me. I want your tender charms. Cause I'm lonely, and I'm blue. I need you and your love, too. C'mon and rescue me." People talk about the aggressive rhythm section on this track. I know that it had some formidable backing musicians such as Maurice White (later the founder and leader of Earth, Wind & Fire) on drums, and a fifteen-year-old Minnie Riperton among the background vocalists.

And oh my gosh, when I heard Jackie Wilson singing "Your Love Keeps Lifting Me Higher," I was over the moon. But Jackie was not the only star on the Brunswick label. Also recording on Brunswick was the fabulous Chi-Lites, led by The Godfather of Vocal Groups, Marshall Thompson. Five years after Jackie's hit, the Chi-Lites recorded their iconic tunes "Have You Seen Her" and "Oh, Girl."

I remember running around the house, singing, "I'm Agent Double-O-Soul, Baby. I'm Agent Double-O-Soul!" But as a youngster I had never heard of Edwin Starr, who would later join Motown and do songs like "25 Miles from Home," and "War (What Is It Good For?)"

It turns out that Edwin was a great songwriter too. He wrote the song, "Oh, How Happy." It was a hit, reaching #12 on the *Billboard* pop chart. It was performed in 1966 by the Shades of Blue, and it was another of my favorite songs.

Everybody has heard of the Godfather of Funk, George Clinton and his Parliament/ Funkadelic groups (two different bands with the same members.) Of them, *Wikipedia* says:

Parliament was originally The Parliaments, a doo-wop vocal group based at a Plainfield, New Jersey barbershop… Clinton was the group leader and manager. The group scored a hit single in 1967 with '(I Wanna) Testify' (co-written by Clinton) on Revilot Records. https://bit.ly/36Zq0Ub

How about that? I was listening to a pre-funk George Clinton on our family Hi-Fi.

Freda Payne? I was utterly in love with one of the prettiest vocalists to grace the music scene, and she had a great song called "Band of Gold." Freda was the older sister of Scherrie Payne, who at one point was a member of the Supremes.

Freda married Gregory Abbot, the singer whose song "Shake You Down," was a smash hit much later.

Few people know that "Band of Gold" was written by Edythe Wayne and Ron Dunbar. Fewer still know that Edythe Wayne and Ron Dunbar were Holland, Dozier, and Holland, writers and producers at Motown who were responsible for many of the Supremes' hits. "Band of Gold" was a significant hit on the Invictus label. (This is the label started by Holland, Dozier, and Holland after they left Motown.)

And who doesn't remember the group called Chairmen of the Board and their hit song, "Give Me Just A Little More Time?" I am sure that my mom and dad got sick and tired of hearing me trying to make my voice crack in that strange, appealing, almost yodeling way of the lead singer, General Johnson, as he performed this song. This group was also on the Invictus label. Need I say more?

Oh my gosh! I just remembered. This article is supposed to be about the Funk Brothers. Had you forgotten too? I am so sorry.

Well, despite what you may be thinking, I have not lost it completely. At least, not yet. *The Saturday Morning Song Chronicles* is about The Funk Brothers, as they were the musicians who played on each of these hit songs and many others for which they never took credit.

I never knew that The Funk Brothers had played on all these non-Motown songs that I loved, and I had to share it with you when I found out.

The Funk Brothers also did some solo projects calling themselves Earl Van Dyke and the Soul Brothers. Some of their recordings like "Soul Stomp," and "Six by Six" became favorites among Northern Soul fans (super fans of American soul music who live in Northern UK and Scotland).

No doubt, the Funk Brothers were the most prolific hit-making unit in the history of music.

And it turns out that I have always been an even bigger Motown Baby than I had believed myself to be.

There are seven carefully curated historical videos listed for your enjoyment below. I hope they bring back some great memories for you, just as they have for me.

***

Referenced Videos:

"Rescue Me"
Fontella Bass
https://bit.ly/3gRSu74

"Cool Jerk"
The Capitols
https://bit.ly/2Xzff8h

"Band of Gold"

Freda Payne
https://bit.ly/3eQ76C8

"Agent Double-O Soul"
Edwin Starr
https://bit.ly/3dy4ad7

"Give Me Just
a Little More Time"
Chairmen of the Board
https://bit.ly/2A06pr1

"Your Love Keeps
Lifting Me Higher"
Jackie Wilson
https://bit.ly/2XxXnu8

"6x6"
Earl Van Dyke
https://bit.ly/3eMKQJi

Chapter 40 – The Andantes

If I asked you to name the most excellent female vocal groups of the 1960s, you would probably come up with names like the Supremes or Martha Reeves and the Vandellas or the Marvelettes or the Ronettes, the Blossoms, the Shangri-Las, or the Shirelles.

But the Andantes? Probably not so much, and yet, the Andantes were perhaps the most gifted and prolific female vocal trio of all time.

The Andantes were to Motown vocals what the Funk Brothers were to Motown music. Artists whose names were never publicized but performed on over 90% of the Motown hits that came out of Detroit before 1972.

The Andantes sang background vocals on over 20,000 Motown songs! If you have ever heard a Motown classic hit from the 1960s, you have listened to the Andantes. "Gifts from God," "heavenly," and "divine" are the terms used by many to describe their vocal gifts. Their names are spoken with reverence to this day by those in the know.

How good were they? If one of The Andantes was ill and could not join the other two in the studio to sing the background vocals together, management shelved the recording project until all three could be present. So, if Stevie Wonder or The Temptations or Marvin Gaye had a hot song going in the studio, they had to wait for the Andantes to sing their background vocals before that record could go forward. With all of the magnificent singers at Motown, what does that tell you about the abilities of the Andantes?

The Andantes had a perfect blend. Blend is the elusive, homogeneous quality that every background vocal group performing everywhere in this world is striving to achieve even now. The Andantes so perfectly executed it that only they could tell who was singing each part. No one else ever could. As a result, the producers at Motown found ways to use the voices of the Andantes that were unprecedented or unusual.

There were times in the studio when the producer would blend the homogenous voices of the Andantes with the lead vocal of the more famous singers they were producing. The Andantes were used to fix a lot of lead vocals, making the "star" sound better than ever.

The Andantes were not promoted by Motown as a performing group, for the same reasons that the Funk Brothers were not. Barry Gordy was protective of the musicians and vocalists he brought together, and he did not want any of them wooed away from his company. If word got out that the Andantes were this phenomenal, any other competing record company would have offered them a contract as lead vocalists making tons more money. The ten dollars a day that they earned from Motown would have been peanuts compared to what others would have paid had they known about the Andantes, and Motown would have lost one of the most significant secret ingredients of their hit-making recipe. After all, The Andantes recorded on a hit record nearly every day at Motown.

Here is a partial list of songs that Jackie Hicks, Marlene Barrow, and Louvain Dempsey, the Andantes, performed on, as provided by *Wikipedia*:

Chart-topping hits: "My Guy" – Mary Wells * "I Can't Help Myself (Sugar Pie Honey Bunch)" – Four Tops * "Reach Out I'll Be There" – Four Tops * "Love Child" – Diana Ross & the Supremes * "I Heard It Through the Grapevine" – Marvin Gaye

The Andantes appeared on many singles for Brenda Holloway. These include: "When I'm Gone" * "Operator" * "You Can Cry on My Shoulder" * "Together 'Til the End of Time" * "Just Look What You've Done"

The Andantes appeared as backing vocalists on 16 singles for the Four Tops. These releases include: "Baby I Need Your Loving" [2] * "Without the One You Love (Life's Not Worth While)" * "Ask the Lonely" * "I Can't Help Myself (Sugar Pie Honey Bunch)" * "It's the Same Old Song" * "Something About You" * "Shake Me, Wake Me (When It's Over)" * "Reach Out I'll Be There" * "Standing in the Shadows of Love" * "Bernadette" * "7-Rooms of Gloom" * "You Keep Running Away" * "I'm in a Different World" * "Still Water (Love)" * "Walk Away Renee" * "If I Were a Carpenter"

They appeared as backing vocalists on eight singles for The Supremes. These releases include: "Children's Christmas Song" * "In and Out of Love" * "Forever Came Today" * "Love Child" [2] * "I'm Livin' in Shame" * "The Composer"

They appeared as backing vocalists on twelve singles for Martha & the Vandellas. These releases include: "You've Been in Love Too Long" * "Love (Makes Me Do Foolish Things)" (B-Side of "You've Been in Love Too Long") * "My Baby Loves Me" (with the Four Tops) * "I'm Ready for Love" * "Jimmy Mack" * "I Promise to Wait My Love" * "Forget Me Not" (B-Side of "I Promise to Wait My Love") * "I Can't Dance to That Music You're Playing" (with Syreeta Wright) * "(We've Got) Honey Love" * "Taking My Love (And Leaving Me)" * "I Should Be Proud"

They appeared as backing vocalists on 14 singles for the Marvelettes. These releases include: "Tie a String Around Your Finger" (B-side of "As Long as I Know He's Mine") "I'll Keep Holding On" * "Don't Mess with Bill" * "You're The One" * "The Hunter Gets Captured by the Game" * "When You're Young and in Love" * "My Baby Must Be a Magician" * "Here I Am Baby" * "Destination: Anywhere" * "What's Easy for Two Is So Hard for One" * "I'm Gonna Hold On As Long As I Can" * "That's How Heartaches Are Made" * "Marionette" * "A Breath-Taking Guy"

They appeared as backing vocalists on five recordings for the Temptations. "It's Growing" * "Last One Out is Broken Hearted" * "Just Another Lonely Night" * "That'll Be the Day" * "Love Woke Me Up This Morning"

They appeared as backing vocalists on (at least) 15 singles for Marvin Gaye. These releases include: "Baby Don't You Do It" * "What Good Am I Without You "* "How Sweet It Is (To Be Loved by You)" * "I'll Be Doggone" * "Pretty Little Baby" * "Ain't That Peculiar" *" One More Heartache" * "Take This Heart of Mine" * "Little Darling (I Need You)" * "Your Unchanging Love" * "I Heard It Through the Grapevine" * "Too Busy Thinking About My Baby" * "That's the Way Love Is" * "The End of Our Road" * "Save the Children"

They also appeared as backing vocalists on these following recordings and singles for Marvin Gaye & Tammi Terrell: "This Poor Heart Of Mine" * "Give In, You Just Can't Win" * "When Love Comes Knocking At My Heart" * "Two Can Have A Party" * "Come On And See Me" * "Oh How I'd Miss You" * "Love Woke Me Up This Morning" [4]

The Andantes have also appeared as backing vocalists on numerous Stevie Wonder recordings, including: "Sunset" (B-side of "Contract on Love") * "Kiss Me Baby" * "Music Talk" (B-side of "Hi-Heel Sneakers") * "Uptight (Everything's Alright)" * "Nothing's Too Good For My Baby" * "A Place in the Sun" * "Hey Love" * "I Was Made to Love Her" * "I'm Wondering" * "Shoo-Be-Doo-Be-Doo-Da-Day" * "For Once in My Life" [2] * "Yester-Me, Yester-You, Yesterday" - https://bit.ly/36ZXfH2

What a resume.

I hope you enjoy the videos that accompany this article. I have curated some of the best examples of the Andantes' background vocals as they supported Motown's great artists.

Join us in two weeks when we share information about a woman who may have been the most exceptional female vocalist of early Motown. I am absolutely convinced that her vocal style and technique was closely emulated by the great Whitney Houston. Music entrepreneur Dick Clark, who hosted the TV show *American Bandstand* for decades, stated before the world that this artist was the greatest vocalist he had ever heard in his entire life.

But next week, hear all about the Originals, another of Motown's secret weapons.

***

Referenced Videos:

"Ain't That Peculiar"
Marvin Gaye
https://bit.ly/3gSGEth

"Reach Out (I'll Be There)"
The Four Tops
https://bit.ly/2ACgZ7G

"Yester-Me, Yester-You,
Yesterday"
Stevie Wonder
https://bit.ly/2MtNyqV

"Love (Makes Me do
Foolish Things)"
Martha Reeves and
the Vandellas
https://bit.ly/30bbE1J

Chapter 41 – The Originals

I remember thinking, *Where have they been hiding?* Their voices were beautiful. Their harmonies were stellar. Teenaged me stood in the living room, mesmerized, listening to the music of this new group, the Originals, now playing on my parents Hi-Fi Stereo.

One of the guys had a voice that reminded me of Melvin Junior of the Dells or David Ruffin of the Temptations. Another had a fantastic, high-flying falsetto voice, and again, those harmonies. *These guys are a little older,* I thought, *so, why haven't I heard of them before?*

The answer to that question was the same as to why precious few of us had ever heard of the Funk Brothers, Motown's in-house studio band or the Andantes, Motown's in-house female vocal trio.

The Originals were another secret weapon of the Motown hit-making factory. They were kept under wraps, used as in-house background vocalists for countless other Motown artists, and, for the most part, just like the Funk Brothers and the Andantes, not promoted as a group themselves.

According to *Wikipedia*:

They recorded the song "Suspicion" in 1966, but it was never released as a single. Nevertheless, it has become a Northern Soul classic. The track has since been featured on many of their compilation albums and many Northern Soul compilations. - https://bit.ly/2XxkbdN

If it was a cut from an album and not a single, KMEN 1290 AM, commonly referred to as K-MEN 129 (pronounced 1-29), our local radio station would never have played it. And in those days, if your single was not broadcast via a brick and mortar radio station, you did not have a record. You had a coaster or a black Frisbee. Either way, nobody in the USA was ever going to hear that song.

Thank God for the Northern Soul movement, located in the northern region of the UK, including Scotland. Many of the not as famous Motown artists and other lesser-known soul artists and their music were embraced by Northern Soul enthusiasts, allowing these artists to experience some measure of success and appreciation of their musical talent and their recordings.

The Northern Soul movement reminded me of college or independent radio stations who played underground music or new music or album cuts. They have forever been adventurous, drawing outside of the lines and helping others to discover great music that was not garden variety or traveling down the beaten path.

But as I was listening to their music in my folk's living room, it was 1969, and things were about to change for the Originals. They had back to back hit singles from two different albums. The songs were named "Baby, I'm For Real" (#1 on *Billboard* magazine's Soul Charts and #14 on *Billboard's* Pop Charts), and "The Bells" (#4 R&B and #12 on the Pop Charts).

Why were the Originals now putting out hit records—achieving something that neither the Funk Brothers nor the Andantes were able to accomplish—after all those years of laboring in anonymity?

These two songs had one thing in common—the great Marvin Gaye.

Marvin Gaye was such a phenomenal vocalist that people forget what a great songwriter he was as well. Marvin co-wrote and produced "Baby, I'm For Real" and "The Bells" for the Originals. And though they had other songs in their career that hit the charts, these two songs would be the only hit records the Originals would ever have, as recording artists.

They, together with the Andantes at times, were the background vocalists on hundreds of Motown songs. However, according to *Wikipedia*, they were the background vocalists on at least nine of my favorite songs of all time. Some of these may have been your favorites too. They are:

1966: "What Becomes of the Brokenhearted" (Jimmy Ruffin; Soul)

1968: "Twenty-Five Miles" (Edwin Starr; Gordy)

1968: "Does Your Mama Know About Me" (Bobby Taylor and the Vancouvers; Gordy)

1968: "Malinda" (Bobby Taylor and the Vancouvers; Gordy)

1968: "For Once in My Life" (Stevie Wonder; Tamla)

1968: "Chained" (Marvin Gaye; Tamla)

1969: "Yester-Me, Yester-You, Yesterday" (Stevie Wonder; Tamla)

1969: "My Whole World Ended (The Moment You Left Me)" (David Ruffin; Motown)

1969: "What Does It Take (To Win Your Love)" (Jr. Walker; Soul)

1970: "War" (Edwin Star; Gordy)

1973: "Just to Keep You Satisfied" (from the album "Let's Get It On"; Marvin Gaye

Tamla)

The Originals were:

Freddie Gorman, Walter Gaines, C.P. Spencer, Hank Dixon, and Joe Stubbs. Stubbs left after less than a year with the group, and Spencer left in 1973 and was replaced by Ty Hunter. – *Discogs* - https://bit.ly/2AGD19q

But time waits for no man. *Wikipedia* adds:

Joe Stubbs, brother of Four Tops lead Levi Stubbs, died on February 5, 1998. He had been with the group [the Originals] for about six months in 1966, as well a member of The Falcons, The Contours, and 100 Proof (Aged In Soul).
C. P. Spencer died on October 20, 2004, and the group's spokesman Freddie Gorman followed on June 13, 2006. Walter Gaines died on January 17, 2012, after a long illness.
Dixon is now the only surviving and active founding member of the original group
Following the death of Freddie Gorman in 2006, longtime member Hank Dixon and Hank's daughter Terrie Dixon reformed The Originals as a live touring act, with Freddie's son songwriter and producer Dillon F. Gorman, plus the son of Gene Chandler, Defrantz Forrest, to complete the line-up. – https://bit.ly/2XxkbdN

The great Jim Gilstrap is now a member of Hank Dixon's touring group of the Originals. Gilstrap has done background vocals for everyone from Dolly Parton to Quincy Jones. He was also a member of Stevie Wonder's backing group, Wonderlove. Do you remember Stevie's Grammy award-winning song, "You Are the Sunshine of My Life"? Then you know the voice of Jim Gilstrap. Jim sings the opening two lines, "You are the sunshine of my life. That's why I'll always be around." Gilstrap's career has been stellar.

The Originals were extraordinary. Please enjoy these historical videos of their hit songs and of some other songs they helped to become hits that we adore.

See you next week for another *Saturday Morning Song Chronicles*.

.

***

Referenced Videos:

"The Bells"
The Originals
https://bit.ly/3hOLKX7

"Baby, I'm For Real"
The Originals
https://bit.ly/2XSvtbe

"What Becomes of
the Brokenhearted"
Jimmy Ruffin
https://bit.ly/2zTabma

"My Whole World Ended"

David Ruffin
https://bit.ly/3dwOarT

"What Does It Take
(To Win Your Love for Me)"
Jr. Walker and the All-Stars
https://bit.ly/2zQUzzC

"Does Your Mama Know About Me"
Bobby Taylor and the Vancouvers
https://bit.ly/3geBY02

Chapter 42 – Brenda Holloway

Music is a subjective thing. We all have our favorite singers and musicians based on the way they move us personally. And I, being a lover of music since I was a child, have been touched by many great artists.

Subjectively speaking, I have stated that for my money, Whitney Houston was the most gifted pop female vocalist of our time. I have also said that Luther Vandross has been the most extraordinary male vocalist of our time. Please don't be mad at me. It is my opinion (and of course I think I am right), so this is my truth. I am sure you have your truth too, and yours may disagree with mine. Don't worry. I won't be mad at you either.

Having long said this about Whitney, just a week ago, as I prepared *The Saturday Morning Song Chronicles*, I had a stunning revelation. It struck me when I started researching a singer I remembered from the past. Her name is Brenda Holloway. I had never seen her perform before. I had only heard her on the radio when I was nine or ten years old. I loved what I heard then, but that is about as far as it went.

During my research, I came across some old videos of Brenda performing on one of the biggest music shows in history, Dick Clark's American Bandstand. If you made it to Bandstand, you had made the big-time.

Brenda Holloway had come long before Whitney Houston, but now seeing these videos and listening to Brenda again as an adult, I could not believe what I was hearing and seeing.

I really could not believe it. I shared a video of Brenda with an extremely talented singer friend of mine to see if she had the same reaction that I had. She did. She stated the very thought that was in my mind that I had left unsaid. She responded, "It's as if someone sat Whitney down and told her to watch Brenda and then sing just like her."

Here was another professional vocalist as stunned as I was at what she had just witnessed on the video.

I have curated a few clips to show you what I mean. Listen to Holloway's vocal runs, and you will remember Whitney making those same vocal runs, perfectly matching Brenda's. Why is that unusual? Because this vocal technique is like a fingerprint, no two vocalists sing vocal runs the same way. They are improvisational, like jazz. To vocalize precisely like someone else, you must listen to that run and practice it to the point of ingraining it into your very being, and then you can do it just so. Truthfully, because of the improvisational nature of vocal runs, even the original singer would be hard-pressed to duplicate one they executed just seconds ago.

I am saying that you must make a concentrated effort to learn that other artists' vocal runs. It is plain as day that this is what Whitney did. She studied Brenda's vocal runs and learned them well.

Listen to how Brenda sings powerfully; then, suddenly, she will sing a line or two very softly, providing a phenomenal contrast. Then, you will remember Whitney doing it just like that too. Whitney even phrased her words and sentences in the same way that Brenda had. I am still shaking my head in disbelief.

But I do think I know what happened. I experienced the same thing as a vocalist. I guess it happens to all singers.

You have someone that you listen to and feel is a great vocalist, and you are inspired. You learn from them. You emulate them, and part of their style becomes part of yours.

Listening to Brenda Holloway, it's clear that Whitney Houston used her as a model or pattern for the way she would sing for the rest of her life.

Why have so many not heard of Brenda Holloway? She (again as was the case with Whitney) was a child prodigy and achieved greatness in her teenage years. Brenda was appearing on Bandstand at seventeen years old, already an accomplished musician who played three instruments (flute, violin, and bass), and sang like no one else in the business. She had hit records at Motown, and there was the expectation that Brenda would become the next Mary Wells.

For whatever reason, Brenda did not get along with management at Motown. It appears she felt that respect was lacking when it came to her talent. Maybe she was right; perhaps she was not. There are two sides to every story, and I have worked with a couple of teenage artists who thought more of themselves than necessary. They made working with them more trouble than it was worth. I have no clue who was in the right and who was in the wrong. Nevertheless, after a few hits on Motown, Brenda Holloway departed the label when she was just 22 years old.

Brenda has been out there on her own all this time. She never reclaimed the success she had in her youth, but, at 73 years of age, she is still singing, looking fabulous, and doing it her way.

Listen to Brenda's hits, "What Are You Going To Do When I'm Gone," "Every Little Bit Hurts," and "I'll Always Love You." Close your eyes, and you may begin to think you are listening to Whitney Houston in several spots.

(Also, isn't it a fantastic coincidence that they each recorded a different song with the same title?)

I hope you enjoy these historical videos, and I think once you have seen and listened to them, you will understand why my highly respected peer said, "It's as if someone sat Whitney down and told her to watch Brenda and then sing just like her."

We all know how great Whitney became. What does it say about Brenda Holloway from whom Whitney obviously learned so much?

By the way, I have a new all-time favorite female vocalist. Her name is Brenda Holloway.

I hope to see you next week for another *Saturday Morning Song Chronicles*.

***

Referenced Videos:

"When I'm Gone"
https://bit.ly/2U6tNtW

"I'll Always Love You"
https://bit.ly/2Xv5Pub

"Every Little Bit Hurts"
https://bit.ly/304Os5i

Chapter 43 – The Ladies in My Life – Part One

I have done many interviews over the years, appearing before millions on TV and the radio. And nearly every interviewer posed the same question. "Who were your musical influences?" The answer to that question is, there have been many.

Today, I am featuring a few of "The Ladies in My Life," those female vocalists whose voices and songs have moved me, inspired me, and made me fall in love with music.

Preferences are subjective. I know you have other female artists who have moved you, but we may have a few in common.

One of the earliest songs that touched my soul was "Our Day Will Come" by Ruby and the Romantics. "Our Day" made me fall in love with mid-tempo ballads. The lyrics and that dreamy arrangement made me sway like a palm tree in the breeze. The background vocals were unusual but gorgeous. I have never heard their like before or since. I fell in love with "Our Day" the very first time I heard it. We are going way back here, so it may be new to some of my younger readers of *The Chronicles*, but if you have not heard it before, you are in for a romantic musical treat.

Then, there was Barbara Lewis. She had two songs that made it onto my all-time favorites list. The first was "Hello Stranger," released in 1963. What makes this great song even more significant is the fact that Barbara, the songwriter, composed it when she was no more than twenty years old.

Another thing that made "Hello Stranger" so different is that the phrase "hello stranger" is only found in the title and the opening line of the song. Add to that it was none other than the legendary Dells who sang background on this song, and you have one for the books.

Van McCoy wrote the Barbara Lewis song I loved the most. We mentioned the same artist and producer in two earlier *Saturday Morning Song Chronicles*. It was Van who brought together Peaches and Herb, and it was he who created one of the biggest dance songs in the history of music, "The Hustle." The tune he wrote that Barbara recorded two years after "Hello Stranger" was called "Baby, I'm Yours." What a gorgeous record.

I was just a kid then, in love with Barbara's great music. I had no idea that one day I would meet her, be on tour with her, and talk to her about how she ended up singing "Baby, I'm Yours."

We (the Platters) were on tour in Hawaii, and Barbara Lewis was also one of the artists on that tour. I vividly remember talking with Barbara inside of the Blaisdell Arena in Honolulu. All the acts were scouting the Blaisdell one day before our scheduled show. The Blaisdell is a unique circular indoor venue. Barbara and I got into a conversation. I told her how much I had always loved her music, and especially "Baby, I'm Yours."

She chuckled and said something to the effect that she did not want to record that song. I could not believe my ears. She said it was a real struggle because she did not feel the song was for her.

Now, keep in mind that Barbara was a great songwriter in her own right. She had written not only "Hello Stranger," but every song on her debut album.

And back in those days, that was the exception, not the rule. If an artist also happened to be a writer, the record company would perhaps allow them to have one or two original songs on the album. The money way back then was in artists doing cover songs, songs that were hit records by other artists, and therefore had a built-in audience. (By the way, the industry has shifted back to that reality again today. Independent artists now make more money by recording and streaming cover songs than writing original content.)

Anyway, Barbara told me that even though she hated doing "Baby, I'm Yours," that she has always been a trooper, and so she dug deep and did her best in the studio. I could see the pride in her eyes as she told me how she had persevered, and especially when she said, "It became my second biggest hit." Well, I loved "Hello Stranger," but Barbara, in my heart, "Baby, I'm Yours" will always be my favorite, and so will you.

Next on my list was a song called "B-A-B-Y" by the Queen of Memphis Soul, Carla Thomas. Thomas was a child prodigy. She was the daughter of radio DJ and recording star Rufus "Walking the Dog" Thomas. She was performing for the public at just ten years old and was signed by Atlantic Records when she was still in high school. Her biggest hit was a song called "Gee Whiz (Look at His Eyes)," which I thought was a beautiful song, but her second-biggest hit, "B-A-B-Y," has always been the one that moved me.

"Hard, cold, and cruel is a man who paid too much for what he got."

What a powerful lyric from the Aretha Franklin song that is not as well known as "R-E-S-P-E-C-T" or "Chain of Fools," or the tune on the flip side of that record, "(Sweet, Sweet Baby) Since You've Been Gone."

But oh, my goodness, this is one of the most soul-wrenching songs that Aretha ever performed, and only she could have pulled it off in such an emotionally compelling way. This song was a family affair, having been written by Aretha's sister, Carolyn.

The record also had background vocals by one of the most prolific backing groups in modern music history, the Sweet Inspirations. Just listen to those beautiful harmonies, and to that ethereal soprano vocal happening behind Aretha's soul-stirring performance. That is the magnificent voice of "Cissy" Houston, the mother of Whitney Houston, and leader of the Sweet Inspirations. Listening to this song is as near a religious experience that one could ever have outside of being in church.

Please enjoy these rare videos.

There are many more musical "Ladies in My Life." I hope you will come back again next week for another *Saturday Morning Song Chronicles* to hear more about them, including an icon who I grew to love and deeply appreciate when we worked together every night for over a month. Her name is Martha Reeves.

***

Referenced Videos:

"Our Day Will Come"
Ruby and the Romantics
https://bit.ly/36YXi61

"Hello Stranger"
Barbara Lewis
https://bit.ly/2Ua8YO7

"Baby, I'm Yours"
Barbara Lewis
https://bit.ly/303MlyJ

"B-A-B-Y"
Carla Thomas
https://bit.ly/2XyYMRw

"Ain't No Way"
Aretha Franklin
https://bit.ly/2XWQDFi

Chapter 44 – The Ladies in My Life – Part Two

I have always loved women. I have always loved beautiful voices. So, the fact that I especially love women with beautiful voices should come as no surprise. I have listened to and learned from some of the most gifted female vocalists in music history. Today, I would like to share some of the songs of more of the phenomenal female artists who helped mold me as a vocalist. I hope you will enjoy "The Ladies in My Life - Part Two."

Linda Jones came like a bolt out of the blue when she sang "Hypnotized." Her voice was so powerful, and her vocal style so very soulful that she just blew everyone away with her delivery of that song. But as I listened to her, with all the power and urgency she sang with, I could feel that she was holding back. I heard her voice and visualized a team of horses pulling a stagecoach; they are about to break free and go into a full gallop. Meanwhile, the poor stagecoach driver clutches the reins with all his might, fighting to keep all heck from breaking loose.

I thought that we would hear hit songs by Linda for many decades to come. I began to wonder why we had not heard more from the woman with an exceptional voice and powerful gymnastic vocal technique. *Wikipedia* answered that question for me:

Shortly after the end of her national tour supporting the album, Jones died at her mother's home at the age of 27 while resting between matinee and evening shows at New York City's Apollo Theater in Harlem. She had been a diabetic for most of her life and slipped into a coma (or more likely, insulin shock) while sleeping. - https://bit.ly/3eMVC21

I hope you will enjoy Linda's signature song, "Hypnotized." As I have, you may imagine what a stellar future she may have experienced, had life been more kind to her.

Because of the attack on Pearl Harbor, December 7, 1941, America went to war. Many babies were born prematurely that day. The attack brought more than physical destruction; it brought waves of anguish and fear.

My Aunt Jackie, I am told, was one of those premature babies born that day. She was the youngest of my mother's siblings, just 12 years old when I was born. My Aunt Jackie loved music. Every time I visited my grandparents, Aunt Jackie, a teenager at the time, played music I had never heard before. It was called R&B. She played "Our Day Will Come" by Ruby and the Romantics and "Any Day Now" by Chuck Jackson. Then, there was "Mockingbird" by Inez and Charlie Foxx.

I never remember seeing this sister and brother act on TV, but during research for *The Saturday Morning Song Chronicles*, I found pictures, and, as the kids of today text, "OMG!" They were gorgeous.

The vocals of this song were so raw and fierce that what I imagined them looking like was a far cry from the truth.

Aunt Jackie, thank you for exposing me to such exciting and beautiful music. I am glad that you were born prematurely and gave us more time to be with you; you left us way too soon.

Betty Everett did a song that I loved. It had the most unusual title. It was called "The Shoop Shoop Song." That had a lot to do with the background vocals, which were another significant part of that tune. Betty's vocal was magnificent. I was ecstatic to find a rare video of her performing this release because I had never seen her before.

The girl group, the Ronettes, seemingly came from nowhere and stormed the American music scene. These three girls had a great song called "Be My Baby," and everyone became a fan.

These young ladies had a style all their own.

Their hairstyles were different, their eye makeup was different, and they seemed so very exotic.

I remember watching them on TV, and I was in love. They were innocent but sexy and just so unlike any other group out there. But as I watched the video that I am sharing with you today, a feeling of déjà vu suddenly hit me, and perhaps it will hit you as well. So far as a look goes, as you watch the Ronettes, think about Amy Winehouse. That is all I am going to say.

And now, I must tell you about working with Martha Reeves and the Vandellas. The Platters, the Coasters, and Martha Reeves and the Vandellas were all together, doing a show six nights a week at the New York, New York Hotel and Casino in Las Vegas, Nevada. Martha is an icon. She was not part of a group; she is the group. The Platters and the Coasters have had many vocalists within their ranks over the years, but Martha Reeves is still Martha Reeves, and still going strong.

Over the month I had the honor of working alongside her on the show, Martha proved to be a gracious and knowledgeable woman, but also a very private person.

For some reason, she liked me, so she spoke to me often about the music business and especially about the kind of things to watch out for in the industry. She is a very astute woman, and all she warned me about came true.

I knew all of Martha's great songs because I was more of a Martha Reeves fan than a Supremes fan. I just felt Martha's songs like "Heatwave" and "Dancing in the Street" had so much more life and fun and energy to them. (Bands all around the world still perform "Heatwave," every night, but which band is playing, "Reach Out and Touch Somebody's Hand"?)

But, researching videos for you today, I learned something about Martha that I never realized before. She and the Vandellas moved and danced so smoothly and soulfully that it is mesmerizing to watch. If Martha never sang a note, I could watch her sway and move to the music all day long. As you watch her videos, see if you don't agree.

It amazes me how *The Saturday Morning Song Chronicles* helps me to see connections that I never saw before, like the Ronettes and Amy Winehouse and Brenda Holloway and Whitney Houston. Now, it is the fact that we had been performing at the New York, New York Hotel and Casino in Las Vegas, Nevada, when the enemy again attacked us on U.S. soil, this time in New York City, New York on September 11th, 2001.

And now, away from the morbid and back to the fun. I have a question for you. Who was the first superstar act of Motown? Was it Stevie Wonder, the Temptations, the Four Tops, Smokey Robinson and the Miracles, The Supremes, Martha Reeves and the Vandellas, Gladys Knight and the Pips, or Marvin Gaye?

If you join me next week for another episode of *The Saturday Morning Song Chronicles,* please be ready for a big surprise.

***

Referenced Videos:

"Be My Baby"
The Ronettes
https://bit.ly/3eGNPD4

"The Shoop Shoop Song"
Betty Everett
https://bit.ly/3dC6jo4

"Hypnotized"
Linda Jones
https://bit.ly/2ByvQAv

"Mockingbird"
Inez and Charlie Foxx
https://bit.ly/3dyq2VM

"Dancing In The Street"
Martha Reeves and the Vandellas
https://bit.ly/3dzBpwx

"Heatwave"
Martha Reeves and the Vandellas
https://bit.ly/2z1AMNg

Chapter 45 – Mary Wells "The Queen of Motown"

The woman who would become known as "The Queen of Motown" had a very rough start in life, and a terrible ending, but in the middle, she created a magic that still lives today.

As a child, Mary Wells contracted spinal meningitis, was partially blind, deaf in one ear, temporarily paralyzed, and had tuberculosis. Now that is a tough first ten years of life. I know I will never complain about being sick again.

Still, just seven years later, she signed a contract with Motown, and, blessed with songs by Smokey Robinson (who also produced her Motown sessions), she had four significant hits. I loved these songs and never realized as a child that they were all done by Mary Wells.

Here are those songs and a little interesting information about each one.

Her first hit song was in 1962 and called, "The One Who Really Loves You." My gosh how I loved this song, and I was a long way from being a teenager at this time, but I think I have always appreciated great music.

And why wouldn't I love it? Smokey Robinson wrote it. The Funk Brothers recorded the music tracks, and Stanford Bracely, Carl Jones, Joe Miles, and Mickey Stevenson sang background vocals as the Love Tones.

This song used a faux calypso rhythm that was super catchy. If you have never heard this song, I think you are about to be delighted.

"The One Who Really Loves You," reached number eight on the *Billboard* Hot 100 chart the week of June 9, 1962.

Following "The One Who Really Loves You" was "You Beat Me to The Punch." Background vocals again by the Love Tones and music by the Funk Brothers. It became a *Billboard* Top 10 Pop smash, peaking at number nine on the pop chart and becoming her first number one hit on the *Billboard* R&B Singles chart. With this one, Mary Wells garnered a Grammy nomination.

Next came the song "Two Lovers." The song became Wells' most successful release to date, reaching number one on the *Billboard* R&B chart and number seven on the *Billboard* Pop chart.

In a rare video of Mary performing "Two Lovers" on a live stage, look very carefully, and you will see something you have perhaps never seen before. It is the Temptations before David Ruffin joined the group, so Otis, Melvin, Paul, and Eddie are singing background vocals for Mary Wells. She was Motown's biggest star at that time. There was a reason they called her "The Queen of Motown." It looks like the Temps were glad to have the gig. There was no question who the megastar was back then.

"My Guy" would become the biggest hit that Mary Wells would ever have, reaching number one on the *Billboard* Hot 100 Pop Singles chart on May 16, 1964.

Here are some fascinating and very cool facts about the recording session of "My Guy," as reported in *Wikipedia*:

At the session for the "My Guy" backing track, the studio musicians were having issues completing the intro: with the musicians having been playing all day and a half-hour scheduled studio time left, trombonist George Bohanon said to keyboardist Earl Van Dyke that the opening measure of "Canadian Sunset" could be perfectly juxtaposed on the intro's chord changes, and Van Dyke, the session bandleader, expediently constructed an intro incorporating the opening of "Canadian Sunset"... Van Dyke would recall: "We were doing anything to get the hell out of that studio. We knew that the producers didn't know nothing 'bout no 'Canadian Sunset'... We figured the song would wind up in the trash can anyway." – https://bit.ly/3dsNqDY

I am presenting a video of the 1956 instrumental hit, "Canadian Sunset," recorded long before Motown existed. Listen to the first few seconds of the song when the piano first comes in, and just before it goes on to play the lead melody line. Then listen to the first measure or two of "My Guy."

Like Artie Johnson of the Laugh-In TV show, you may say, "Very in-te-rest-ing..." For those of you who have no idea of which I speak, there is a video.

And didn't you love the way Mary ended her vocals on "My Guy"? The way she spoke in a choppy, sexy way rather than singing those last words? It became one of my favorite parts of the song. Maybe yours too.

Wikipedia tells us what that was all about as well.

When Wells recorded her vocal, she sang over the song's outro with a huskiness evoking the line delivery of Mae West: Wells would recall: "I was only joking but the producers said 'Keep it going, keep it going.'" - https://bit.ly/3dsNqDY

I have a rare video clip of Mae West, one of Hollywood's first sex symbols of the silver screen, visiting the U.K. Listen as she says to her interviewer, "Why don't you come up and see me some time," (this was one of her famous catchphrases). When you hear that, you will instantly recognize that Mary was playfully imitating Mae's style and delivery as she played around in the studio. Mary's kidding around ended up on one of the most excellent records of all time.

"My Guy" would be the last hit single Mary Wells, "The Queen of Motown," would record for the company. Mary learned that money earned from "My Guy" was being used to promote the Supremes' latest single, "Where Did Our Love Go." That was the straw that broke the camel's back for her.

Mary had signed her contract with Motown when she was seventeen, so she could get out of it and sign with another company once she turned twenty-one years old.

Mary would continue to record but never again have the level of success that she achieved with Motown. The last part of her life ended as it had begun, with her extremely ill and dying at the age of forty-nine.

Thanks for being here again with us today. See you next weekend for another *Saturday Morning Song Chronicles* as we begin to examine the career of the great Smokey Robinson.

***

Referenced Videos:

"The One Who Really Loves You"
https://bit.ly/3dygiuE

"You Beat Me to The Punch"
https://bit.ly/3dK2GwB

"Two Lovers"
https://bit.ly/3gWA70W

"My Guy"
https://bit.ly/371Y0zf

"Canadian Sunset"
Eddie Heywood
Hugo Winterhalter
https://bit.ly/2XZq56f

Mae West Interview – 1947
https://bit.ly/2AGFZe4

Very Interesting – Arte Johnson –
Rowan & Martin's Laugh-In
https://bit.ly/2zPQU53

Chapter 46 - Smokey Robinson – The Performer

As a performer, Smokey Robinson has provided us with over fifty years of musical miracles. We most strongly associate Smokey with Barry Gordy Jr. of Motown fame, but Smokey was working with Barry, even before there was a Motown.

The Miracles, with Smokey Robinson as the lead vocalist, was one of the first acts to be signed to the company. Smokey soon gave Motown its first million-selling record with a Smokey Robinson / Barry Gordy written tune called "Shop Around." I hope you enjoy the rare video of the group performing this song.

From 1960 to 1970, the Smokey produced hits of the Miracles were many. They had 26 Top Ten hits. Here is a partial list:

"You've Really Got a Hold On Me" * "Mickey's Monkey" * "I Second That Emotion" * "Baby, Baby Don't Cry" * Ooh Baby, Baby" * "Going to a Go-Go" * "The Tracks of My Tears" * "(Come Round Here) I'm The One You Need" * "The Love I Saw in You Was Just a Mirage" * and "More Love." And then there was the group's only number one hit record while Smokey was with them, "The Tears of a Clown."

Now, remember, this was only between 1960 and 1970.

Smokey left the Miracles in the early 1970s and took an administrative role at Motown, but he resurfaced a year later as a solo act.

It did not go well for him at first, but in 1973 Smokey wrote the lyrics to a Marv Tarplin tune, and it became Smokey's first solo Top Ten Pop Single. It was called "Cruisin.'" According to *Wikipedia,*

"Crusin'" …hit number one in Cash Box magazine and peaked at number four on the *Billboard* Hot 100. It also became his first solo number one in New Zealand." – https://bit.ly/3cxTDgP

Smokey was still around and doing great things in the 1980s as well. Do you recall these songs?

"Being with You" (number two on the *Billboard* Hot 100 chart and number one on the U.K. Singles chart) * "Just to See Her" and "One Heartbeat" (both Top Ten on *Billboard's* Pop, Soul, and Contemporary charts).

By this time, Smokey had been turning out hits for 30 years!

Since that time, Smokey has continued to put out great music, though not all of it has been as successful as his earlier hit songs. And, from 2000 to 2020, Smokey is still active.

Your children and grandchildren, and perhaps even your great-grandchildren may be listening to Smokey as we speak. How? He is the artist singing the opening credits to a show made for little kids called Toddworld.

Smokey has always been, is, and will always be, fresh and relevant. In 2019, at the age of 79, Smokey sang background vocals on the track of one of my favorite young artists, Anderson .Paak. The name of the song is "Make It Better." And you will love the video recorded when Smokey got on stage with Paak, and they sang it together on Jimmy Kimmel Live!

Smokey is in the Rock and Roll Hall of Fame and has won every award in music you could imagine, including four Grammys, two of which are Grammy Legend Awards he received in different years, and one Lifetime Achievement Grammy.

But, to my way of thinking, Smokey has won two other awards that show what a tremendous impact he and his music have made on a universal level.

In December 2006, Smokey Robinson was one of five Kennedy Center honorees, including Dolly Parton, Zubin Mehta, Steven Spielberg, and Andrew Lloyd Webber. Now that is a high-powered line-up.

And, in 2016 Smokey was awarded the 2016 Library of Congress Gershwin Prize for his lifetime contributions to popular music.

One last question. Have you ever wondered how William Robinson Jr. got the nickname "Smokey"? Smokey answered that question for us in an article found in *Wikipedia*:

My Uncle Claude was my favorite uncle; he was also my godfather. He and I were really, really close. He used to take me to see cowboy movies all the time when I was a little boy because I loved cowboy movies. He got a cowboy name for me, which was Smokey Joe. So from the time I was three years old if people asked me what my name was I didn't tell them my name was William, I told them my name was Smokey Joe. That's what everyone called me until I was about 12 and then I dropped the Joe part. I've heard that story about him giving it to me because I'm a light-skinned Black man but that's not true. - https://bit.ly/2UbS81r

And there you have it.

On February 19th, William "Smokey" Robinson Jr. will turn 80 years old. Smokey, we love you, and we wish you at least 80 more great years of making music that will continue to change the world.

Enjoy all of the rare videos today, and as a bonus, enjoy a super-rare Smokey and the Miracles video with them doing a medley that finishes in one of the most beautiful versions of the Beatles' song, "Yesterday" that I have ever heard. Indeed, this is Smokey at his best.

Smokey Robinson has left an indelible mark on the world of music as a performer. Join me next week when I will share with you the fact that in the case of Smokey Robinson and the true measure of his impact on the world of music, what we learned today is only the tip of the iceberg.

***

Referenced Videos:

"Shop Around"

Smokey Robinson
and the Miracles
https://bit.ly/30KtaKJ

"Ooh Baby Baby"
Smokey Robinson
and the Miracles
https://bit.ly/3067Pee

"The Tears of a Clown"
Smokey Robinson
and the Miracles
https://bit.ly/3cxWiXR

"Crusin'"
Smokey Robinson
https://bit.ly/2MFRq8B

"One Heartbeat"
Smokey Robinson
https://bit.ly/3cEdLhn

"Toddworld Theme Song"
Smokey Robinson
https://bit.ly/3gVlgU6

"Make It Better"
Anderson .Paak
featuring Smokey Robinson
https://bit.ly/2XwEKXR

"Yesterday"
Smokey Robinson

and the Miracles

https://bit.ly/370eQ1z

Chapter 47 – Smokey Robinson – The Songwriter

The most venerable music magazine in the world, next to *Billboard* magazine, is called *Rolling Stone*. To even have your name mentioned in either of those journals is something that most of the songwriters on this planet will never achieve.

So, when *Rolling Stone* published an article named "The 100 Greatest Songwriters of All Time," you can bet that the music world stood up and took notice. You can also bet that the people named on that list are considered songwriting royalty.

Otis Blackwell, the songwriter that we featured in *The Saturday Morning Song Chronicles* several months ago, came in at number 98, one notch behind Taylor Swift at number 97, who was one notch behind the songwriting team of Timberland and Missy Elliot, who came in at number 98.

One of my all-time favorite artists and songwriters, Babyface, came in at number 90: and, though we think of him more as an artist than a songwriter, a friend of my grandparents, Mr. Sam Cooke, came in at number 86.

Motown greats Ashford & Simpson came in at number 83, and Marvin Gaye came in at number 82.

Over at Stax Records, the songwriting team of Isaac Hayes and David Porter came in at number 75. A few of the songs they penned, like "Hold On (I'm Coming)" and "Soul Man," demonstrated that they were a dynamic duo, to be sure.

And another dear friend of my grandparents, Paul and Dorothy Allen of Omaha, Nebraska, came in at number 72. His name was Fats Domino.

Look at these great songwriters and all the phenomenal songs they gifted this world, and we are not even down to number 70 yet. How extraordinary a songwriter you would have to be to make the top ten of this list. I'm sure you have guessed that our subject for this week, Smokey Robinson, has done just that. Smokey came in as the number five all-time greatest songwriter in music history.

But, in Smokey's case, *Rolling Stone* added one particularly important fact. Here is what they said about him:

"The melodic and lyrical genius behind Motown's greatest hits is the most influential and innovative R&B tunesmith of all time."

Wow! Number five in pop music, and the most influential writer to ever grace R&B music.

Sir Paul McCartney of the Beatles, who is second on this list, said this about Smokey as a songwriter:

"Smokey Robinson was like God in our eyes."

And Bob Dylan—named the greatest songwriter in music history—said that Smokey Robinson was "The greatest living poet." - https://bit.ly/2XuXBSU

When Dylan and McCartney speak with such reverence about Smokey Robinson, what does that tell you?

Let's evaluate on our own and see if we agree with *Rolling Stone*, Sir Paul, and Bob Dylan.

Here is a partial list of songs written by Smokey Robinson according to the website Songfacts:

"Ain't That Peculiar" - Marvin Gaye
"Bad Girl" - The Miracles
"Don't Mess With Bill" - The Marvelettes

"Floy Joy" - The Supremes

"Get Ready" - The Temptations

"Going To A Go-Go" - The Miracles

"Got a Job" - The Miracles

"I'll Be Doggone" - Marvin Gaye

"I'll Try Something New" - The Supremes

"My Girl" - The Temptations

"My Guy" - Mary Wells

"Since I Lost My Baby" - The Temptations

"The Composer" - The Supremes

"The One Who Really Loves You" - Mary Wells

"The Tracks Of My Tears" - The Miracles

"The Way You Do The Things You Do" - The Temptations

"Two Lovers" - Mary Wells

"Way Over There" - The Miracles

"Who's Lovin' You" - The Jackson 5

"You Beat Me to the Punch" - Mary Wells

"You've Really Got A Hold On Me" - The Miracles

"Your Heart Belongs To Me" - The Supremes

- https://bit.ly/2Y3OEyY

Well, there is no doubt. Even though William "Smokey" Robinson Jr. has made a tremendous impact on the world of music as a performer, his greatest legacy and gift to this world will be the songs that he has written.

The rare videos this week are something. We have the Supremes and the Temptations together singing Smokey's "I'll Try Something New." Out of all the songs I have ever loved by the Jackson 5, the Smokey tune, "Who's Loving You" showed me most clearly what a great singer Michael Jackson was. You singers out there know what I mean.

And check out the Temptations performing "My Girl" and "Get Ready" on the same video. I think that "Get Ready" displays not only what great vocalists they were, but also what phenomenal dancers they were. Their dance routines were the best: second to none.

There is another Temptations video, as well. It is one of my favorites, because Paul Williams, the first gravelly-voiced singer of the Temptations, is singing lead. Soon, David Ruffin would take the lead singing "My Girl," and Paul's days of singing lead would be over, and his downward spiral would soon end his life.

Brenda Holloway was one of Motown's most gifted female vocalists of all time, and it is my pleasure to present her singing another great Smokey tune, "When I'm Gone."

I hope you enjoy Marvin Gaye singing Smokey's "Ain't That Peculiar?" and that you will smile when you hear Bobby Taylor and the Vancouvers performing "Malinda," another Smokey Robinson classic.

As always, *The Saturday Morning Song Chronicles* presents me with a new personal revelation. Today, it is this. My singing a Smokey Robinson song at a karaoke place directly led to my joining the Platters. How about that for a revelation?

I had a video recording cut as I sang at Ellis Island Hotel and Casino, a well-known karaoke spot in Las Vegas, Nevada. I performed what has always been my favorite Temptations' song, "Since I Lost My Baby." It was not until this morning that I realized Smokey wrote this song. A few people saw the video and recommended me to the Platters, and the rest is history.

I have a clip of that video, and though the sound has degraded with time, I thought you might like to see and hear me perform the Smokey Robinson tune that changed my life. I never knew that anyone would see it, other than a few music industry professionals. It was a video "calling card," as I attempted to gain access to the music scene in Las Vegas.

Smokey, all I can say is, "Thank you." The difference you and your music have made in my life is profound. Millions of music fans around the world say the same.

And I thank all of you for hanging with us these past two weeks as we talked about the dual career of the magnificent artist and songwriter, Smokey Robinson, who will turn 80 years old in just a few days. What a national treasure he has proven to be.

We look forward to seeing you next week at *The Saturday Morning Song Chronicles* when we talk about "The Forgotten Stars of Motown."

***

Referenced Videos:

"Who's Loving You"
The Jackson 5
https://bit.ly/2MuV9FC

"My Girl" / "Get Ready"
The Temptations
https://bit.ly/2XykJQx

"Ain't That Peculiar"
Marvin Gaye
https://bit.ly/2U9c19s

"Try Something New"
Diana Ross and the Supremes
The Temptations
https://bit.ly/3gOOy70

"When I'm Gone"
Brenda Holloway
https://bit.ly/2U6tNtW

"Malinda"
Bobby Taylor and
the Vancouvers
https://bit.ly/2XWY0ws

"I Want A Love I Can See"
The Temptations
(featuring Paul Williams)
https://bit.ly/3dzhn5c

"My Guy"
Mary Wells
https://bit.ly/371Y0zf

"Since I Lost My Baby"
Paul B Allen III – Ellis Island
https://bit.ly/30elPm2

Chapter 48 – Forgotten Stars of Motown

We all know Stevie Wonder, Diana Ross, the Supremes, the Temptations, Smokey Robinson, the Miracles, Martha Reeves and the Vandellas, Marvin Gaye, Gladys Knight and the Pips, the Four Tops, Mary Wells, and the Jackson 5. They are pretty much household names.

But did you know that Motown had other artists, ones that precious few of us have even known about? And those of us who once knew that these artists were with Motown have probably forgotten by now. This subject fascinated me, and I think you may be pretty interested too.

So, who are these performers? Well, have you ever seen the movie *Die Hard*? How about the 1985 television series, *Moonlighting*? Does the movie *Pulp Fiction* ring a bell? Yes, we are talking about the actor Bruce Willis. Did you know that he was an artist with Motown at one time, with groups like the Temptations doing background vocals on his songs? I have a video I think you are going to love; June Pointer of the Pointer Sisters joins Bruce Willis on the tune, "Respect Yourself." The previous smash hit by the Staple Singers became a hit once again, this time going to number five on the *Billboard* Hot 100 Chart.

And then there was the gorgeous and talented Barbara McNair, one of the first black women on television. She even hosted the variety TV program, *The Barbara McNair Show*, which ran from 1969 to 1971. Barbara was already an established singer and performer by the time she signed with Motown in 1965. Between 1965 and 1968, she recorded nearly 50 songs with Motown, but more than half of them were never released. Today, I share an old and rare video of this beautiful star singing before a live TV audience. The name of the song, which was her biggest hit in America, is "You're Gonna Love My Baby."

However, Barbara also recorded a song in 1966 called "Baby A-Go-Go." Berry Gordy did not care for this song, so it was never released. Years later, bootlegged copies made it to the U.K., and the song became a massive Northern Soul hit. (The Northern Soul Movement consisted of people located in the northern part of the U.K. and Scotland. These folks loved the lesser-known Motown artists and other soul music artists of the 1960s and 1970s.) Motown finally gave "Baby A-Go-Go" a proper release, but not until the year 2002, nearly 40 years after recording it, and just five years before Barbara died. I am so happy she got to see her song become a big hit in the U.K. She had to feel vindicated after all that time.

Then there is Kiki Dee, the first white U.K. artist ever to be signed to Motown. Shortly after that, Kiki teamed up with Sir Elton John for "Don't Go Breakin' My Heart." But before she departed Motown, she had a hit song in America, a sultry cover of the song "Love Makes the World Go Round." She also had the substantial Northern Soul hit, "The Day Will Come Between Sunday and Monday."

Now, we all know Frankie Valli of Frankie Valli and the Four Seasons. He and they were famous long before Frankie signed with Motown. Frankie only signed with Motown because he was under the impression that Berry Gordy himself would take a hands-on approach in working with him. But Berry was so involved with Diana Ross, and the Motown film Lady Sings the Blues at that time, that Frankie did not feel that Berry delivered on their arrangement. Still, Frankie also had a big Northern Soul hit with his Motown recorded song, "The Night."

I am sure Frankie was frustrated with Motown and Berry for another reason, though for him, it turned out to be a blessing in disguise.

While still an artist with Motown, Frankie recorded the song that would be his biggest solo hit, "My Eyes Adored You." Berry Gordy was not thrilled with the song, so Motown never released it. When Frankie's contract was up, he paid Motown $4,000 for the rights to the song and the master recording, and then he got the song to a different record company; within a few months, it was the number one hit in America and found huge success worldwide.

And here is one for the books. Bobby Darrin signed with Motown Records and recorded one or two albums worth of material. But he died soon after, and his songs were "shelved" (unreleased) and forgotten about until decades later. I am sharing two of those songs with you today, and you can tell they could have been hits had they been released back then. Even Smokey Robinson still believes that to this day.

Here is one clarifying note. I was born in Omaha, Nebraska, a mid-western state. So, I had never heard the southern expression, "The Devil must be beating his wife."

I researched this expression. The phrase describes the phenomenon of rain falling while the sun is still shining: rainfall on a sunny day. Knowing this makes it much easier to understand what Bobby Darrin is trying to convey in one of today's videos.

Under Motown tutelage, this is not the same Bobby Darrin you remember hearing sing "Mack the Knife" or "Splish Splash, I Was Taking A Bath."

Life takes all of us, even the stars of the musical firmament, on convoluted journeys. But, if we are going to play the game, we must take the cards we're dealt and make the best hand we can make.

I've got my fingers crossed. I hope to see you again next week for another *Saturday Morning Song Chronicles*.

***

Referenced Videos:

"Under the Boardwalk"
Bruce Willis with the Temptations
https://bit.ly/3cBtmxP

"Save the Last Dance for Me"
Bruce Willis
https://bit.ly/2Uaidhh

"You're Gonna Love My Baby"
Barbara McNair
https://bit.ly/2A3XpB4

"Baby A Go-Go"
Barbara McNair

https://bit.ly/376goqT

"The Night"
Frankie Valli and
the Four Seasons
https://bit.ly/2Y2bqau

"My Eyes Adored You"
Frankie Valli and the
Four Seasons
https://bit.ly/36YbZWQ

"Love Makes the World Go Round"
Kiki Dee
https://bit.ly/3gZgipN

"The Day Will Come Between
Sunday and Monday"
Kiki Dee
https://bit.ly/3cBum53

"The Devil Must Be Beating
His Wife"
Bobby Darrin
https://bit.ly/2MpHHTw

"Child of Tears"
Bobby Darrin
https://bit.ly/3dzrA1x

Chapter 49 – Burt Bacharach

I was thinking about the music of my youth that inspired me, and I immediately thought about Chuck Jackson, and his beautiful song, "Any Day Now."

Then, I thought about the magnificent Jerry Butler. What a voice: So beautiful and distinctive. The song he did that touched my soul was "Make It Easy on Yourself."

It was not until I started to research these songs that I discovered that the same man co-wrote them both. I was stunned. Burt Bacharach?

I knew the many songs that Burt had done with Dionne Warwick. I have always felt that the marriage of her voice with his music was pure magic. Burt accounted for nearly all of Dionne's early hits. There was "Don't Make Me Over," "Wishin' and Hopin,'" "Anyone That Had A Heart," "Walk On By," "A House Is Not A Home," "You'll Never Get To Heaven If You Break My Heart," "I Say A Little Prayer," "Always Something There to Remind Me," and "Do You Know The Way To San Jose."

But these soul classics by Chuck Jackson and Jerry Butler were nothing like the Dionne Warwick songs. I wondered, are there other songs I have loved over the years, but never realized Burt Bacharach had written them?

I am still shaking my head at what I discovered, and I must share it with you. There were so many mega-hits, and they are so diverse that it boggled my mind.

These were songs I grew up listening to and loving. How did I not know that the same man wrote them all? I think you will be as stunned as I was when you see these song titles. You may have thought the groups themselves were the composers of many of these tunes. I know I did. I was wrong. Here is the list:

The Shirelles – "Baby, It's You"
The Carpenters – ("They Long to Be) Close To You"
Dusty Springfield – "The Look of Love"
Herb Alpert – "This Guy's in Love with You"
The Fifth Dimension – "One Less Bell to Answer"
B.J. Thomas – "Raindrops Keep Falling On My Head"
D. Warwick, S. Wonder, Elton John, Gladys Knight – "That's What Friends Are For"
Jerry Butler – "Make It Easy On Yourself"
Chuck Jackson – "Any Day Now"

And there are so many others.

One thing you may be thinking about now is that other artists did some of the songs mentioned. For instance, Aretha Franklin made "Answer My Prayer" her own, no ifs, ands, or buts about it. Still, Dionne Warwick did it first and did it well. Luther Vandross did a number on "A House is Not a Home." No one will ever come close to doing the song in the way that he did. There is a video that shows Luther singing this song as Dionne Warwick watches and listens. You can see that even though she was the first person to sing this song—and she did have a hit with it—she is nearly overwhelmed listening to Luther's version. It is moving. Watch Dionne (and the rest of the crowd) as he performs it. You and I can argue until the cows come home, but I will always feel that Luther Vandross was the quintessential male vocalist of our lifetime.

But that is one of the signs of a great song; that others can take it, make it their own, and allow the song to become a hit all over again.

These are the kinds of songs that Burt Bacharach writes.

Enjoy these rare videos and the magic of Burt Bacharach. His music has graced us forever, even if we did not realize that these musical gifts came from him.

See you next week for another installment of *The Saturday Morning Song Chronicles*.

***

Referenced Videos:

"Any Day Now"
Chuck Jackson
https://bit.ly/3gLN5OK

"Make It Easy
On Yourself"
Jerry Butler
https://bit.ly/3cw2jnJ

"They Long to Be
Close to You"
The Carpenters
https://bit.ly/2U93YsS

"Walk on By"
Dionne Warwick
https://bit.ly/30dEdfb

"A House is not
a Home"

Luther Vandross
https://bit.ly/2WWxvHS

"The Look of Love"
Dusty Springfield
https://bit.ly/2Y2ddMK

"I Say a Little
Prayer for You"
Aretha Franklin
https://bit.ly/3cAvFkO

"One Less Bell to Answer"
The Fifth Dimension
https://bit.ly/2MvjkEa

"Raindrops Keep
Fallin' On My Head"
B.J. Thomas
https://bit.ly/2XxOf9e

"That's What Friends Are For"
Dionne Warwick
Stevie Wonder
Sir Elton John
Gladys Knight
https://bit.ly/2Y2JvXR

Chapter 50 – "La La Peace Song"

At the beginning of each new week, I have no idea what *The Saturday Morning Song Chronicles* will be about; I keep my eyes and ears open and let the universe become the muse that guides me.

This week, on the site of a dear friend, I saw a post that she had created. She was talking about a "song that she couldn't stop dancing to," and she was kind enough to post a link to that song.

That dear friend is musical artist Larissa Larissa, leader of the exciting Larissa Larissa Band. She is also the owner of that angelic soprano voice you hear singing background vocals when she's on tour with the legendary Chi-Lites featuring Marshall Thompson. Mr. Thompson is rightfully called by all in the music industry, "The Godfather of Vocal Groups."

My mouth dropped open the moment I saw Larissa's post because I have a strong connection with this song. Not that I wrote it or performed on it, but another of my dear friends had.

However, there is more to this story. The version of the song that Larissa posted, I had never heard before and did not know existed.

The name of the song is "La La Peace Song," by the great O.C. Smith.

I have been called "The Professor" and the "Musical Archeologist" by two of my most beloved readers of *The Chronicles*. (Thank you, Joey. Thank you, Larissa.)

I so enjoy the fact that they see me in this light (even though I know there is a fair bit of teasing that comes along with my honorary titles).

But I see myself as more of a "Musical Detective." When I spot a musical mystery, I'm on it. I have an intense natural curiosity, and so I am driven to find answers. If those answers are interesting enough, I love sharing them with you.

When people ask me what I do for fun, I tell them this is it.

Also, I am a little bit OCD when it comes to getting answers to questions that are burning in my mind, because—well—they feel as if they are literally burning in my mind. So, there's that.

When I saw a version of "La La Peace Song" that I did not know, I immediately started giving myself the third degree. *When did O. C. Smith do this song? I thought Al Wilson did it first. Did he? Who had the better version? Why do I know Al's version but not O.C. Smith's? What's the difference between the two, arrangement-wise. What's the story here, anyway?*

I set about to find the answers.

First, I found that the song was written by neither Al Wilson nor by O.C. Smith, but by another great singer. It was written by singer/ songwriter/producer Johnny "Hang on in There, Baby" Bristol.

And here are some remarkably exciting connections:

Johnny Bristol, the writer of the song, produced both the O.C. Smith version on Columbia (which later became Sony) and the Al Wilson version over at Bell Records.

Later, Bell Records became Arista Records, a part of Columbia, and Clive Davis, the new chief of Arista, continued to perform the same magic at Arista that he had done at Columbia for so many years.

Both O.C. and Al Wilson were famous before they did "La La Peace Song." O.C. had a hit called "Little Green Apples," and another called "The Son of Hickory Holler's Tramp," which killed in the U.K. but was banned by many radio stations in the USA because of the lyrical content of the song. But I must tell you, every time I hear "The Son of Hickory Holler's Tramp," it brings tears to my eyes and a lump to my throat. Man, what a song! Talk about keeping it real? Please enjoy the referenced video.

And before he sang his version of "La La Peace Song," Al had "Show and Tell." (Al would also do the song "The Snake," which is the number four most popular song in the history of the Northern Soul Movement.)

So, both artists had smash hits in America and with the Northern Soul Movement in the U.K.

O.C. put out "La La Peace Song" in 1973, but Columbia did not like the record, so they did not promote it, basically "shelving" it.

In 1974 at Bell Records, they believed that Al could have a hit with that song. They did a "cover" version and released it, and it started moving up the charts.

But, when Columbia saw how well the song was doing for him (Al's version broke the Top 40 and peaked at #30 on the charts), they re-released O.C. Smith's version. It did not crack the Top 40 but peaked at #62. The result was that neither of the versions reached their full potential. It was like they canceled each other out, which was indeed a shame.

I was spending a lot of time in Hollywood. That is when Al and I became friends and hung out in L.A. One day, Al handed me a copy of his new album, *La La Peace Song*, named for the "A-side" single of the album.

After my research and jogging my memory, freeing it from the cobwebs (I haven't thought of "La La Peace Song" or the circumstances surrounding it in over forty years), the answers started coming. Here is what I pieced together.

I never heard O.C. Smith's version because Columbia did not promote it in 1973. I heard Al's release in 1974 because Al had given me a copy of the album.

When Columbia quickly released the O.C. Smith version, just as Al's version was gaining traction and on pace to be a huge hit, the records canceled each other out.

Since O.C.'s version never achieved "hit" (Top 40 status), you would rarely hear it on the radio because most stations played only the top 40 hits. Therefore, the chance of hearing Al's version on the radio was far greater than hearing O.C.'s version.

Which version is better?

Both O.C. and Al were excellent vocalists; for this song, I prefer Al's more polished voice and delivery. But Larissa Larissa mentioned in her post that she "couldn't stop dancing" to the song. She was enjoying O.C. Smith's version.

Indeed, the arrangement of that release has a more upbeat tempo, a disco beat, a lightly infused island music flavor, and is engaging, appealing, infectious, and just plain fun. Even if you have two left feet, this song makes you want to get up and dance.

Whichever version you like the best, you can't go wrong. If you want to dance, choose O.C. Smith's version. If you're going to contemplate the message of the song, listen to Al's version.

The bottom line is, Larissa Larissa, you know your stuff.

In closing, I would like to draw your attention to one thing. There is so much more to music than meets the eye (or ear). Too many times, it is about the business of music rather than the music itself.

LL, thanks for the inspiration. This week's *Chronicles* lives because of you.

Enjoy these rare videos, and please join me next week for another installment of *The Saturday Morning Song Chronicles*. Let's see which musical mystery the muse will lead us to solve when we are together next.

***

Referenced Videos:

"La La Peace Song"
O.C. Smith
https://bit.ly/2UbEMC6

"La La Peace Song"
Al Wilson
https://bit.ly/2U74GH6

"Hang on in There,
Baby"
Johnny Bristol
https://bit.ly/2Y3TwUM

"The Son of
Hickory Holler's Tramp"
O.C. Smith
https://bit.ly/3096Iuu

"Show and Tell"

Al Wilson
https://bit.ly/3gSwI3a

"Little Green Apples"
O.C. Smith
https://bit.ly/2U9vsig

"The Snake"
Al Wilson
https://bit.ly/2XxnSjr

Chapter 51 – Not Supposed to be Hits

Things change. One of my favorites sayings is, "The only thing that will never change is that things are going to change." And though the powers that be try to convince us that things are always changing for the better, sometimes, that is not the case.

When I was a boy, the caramel in Milk Duds was softer and covered in real milk chocolate. Talk about delicious? Still, they were messy, for sure. On a warm day, the chocolate covered my fingers. But what fun it was to suck the chocolate off after I had eaten the last Milk Dud.

Today, the caramel in Milk Duds is "covered with a confectionery coating made from cocoa and vegetable oil." - *Wikipedia*. Milk Duds - https://bit.ly/2Uaclo7

Yikes! Sucking vegetable oil from your fingertips doesn't sound nearly as appealing.

The only reason one would argue that Milk Duds are delicious now is that they do not know how great they used to be.

Today, when it comes to music, you may think you are getting a good deal, being able to download a single (one song) for 99 cents from iTunes, and other distributors all around the world. But this is another area where the change has not been for the better. When I was growing up, you could buy a single for a buck as well, but you did not get only one song. You got two songs for that one buck. Check that. You got one song and one mystery.

When vinyl records were all the rage initially (because they are all the rage again now), the singles would have what was called the A-side and the B-side. The A-side was the main song that the record companies wanted for the radio DJs to play on air. The B-side was usually a throw-away song, something to fill that other side of the single—and by design—placed there to avoid being competitive with side A. And, in most cases, the plan worked. Many B-sides were terrible.

But I was intrigued by the mystery of the B-side because many times, there were hidden gems, and who doesn't like discovering buried treasure?

Record companies made mistakes. The A-side was often not the hit they thought it would be, and at some point, the single would be considered a failure: a dud. (Do you see what I did there?) Then it would be dropped from radio airplay altogether. But sometimes, DJs would let their curiosity get the better of them, and they would take a listen to side B, and perhaps find a piece of beautiful magic to share with the world.

Today, we will look at single vinyl records and first examine the A-sides, which we were supposed to hear on the radio, but probably did not. Then we will listen to the B-sides, which we were never supposed to hear on the air, but became classics heard by millions.

Check out Ben E. King singing the A-side single, "First Taste of Love," and then its iconic B-side smash hit, "Spanish Harlem."

Listen to Smokey Robinson sing "Happy Landing," then its hit on side B, "You Really Got a Hold on Me."

The Spinners had a double-sided hit. On the A-side, you may recognize "How Could I Let You Get Away," but I'm sure you will agree that side B, "I'll Be Around," was a much bigger hit. Still, you will most certainly enjoy the performance of the great Philippé Wynne on the A-side. He was another phenomenal talent taken way too soon.

And perhaps the most excellent example of what we are talking about today is that of powerhouse vocalist Gloria Gaynor. Listen to what was supposed to be her hit record, called "Substitute," but then marvel at one of the most performed songs of all time, the B-side mega-hit, "I Will Survive."

I miss licking the chocolate from my fingers after consuming a box of Milk Duds, and I do long for the sense of discovery that I used to enjoy when single records had two sides.

Have fun with these rare videos, and I hope to see you here at *The Saturday Morning Song Chronicles* again next week.

***

Referenced Videos:

"First Taste of Love"
Ben E. King
https://bit.ly/2XYUr98

"Spanish Harlem"
Ben E. King
https://bit.ly/2UbZnq9

"Happy Landing"
Smokey Robinson
https://bit.ly/2XYt5A2

"You Really Got
a Hold on Me"
Smokey Robinson
https://bit.ly/2Xurl2q

"How Could I Let You
Get Away"
The Spinners
https://bit.ly/370dHXO

"I'll Be Around"
The Spinners
https://bit.ly/3dz7vbV

"Substitute"
Gloria Gaynor
https://bit.ly/2ACwwEw

"I Will Survive"
Gloria Gaynor
https://bit.ly/3084M56

Chapter 52 – And in This Corner...

There have been some historic match-ups throughout the ages. David vs. Goliath, Cassius Clay (later named Muhammad Ali) vs. Sonny Liston, the Boston Celtics vs. the Los Angeles Lakers, the Boston Red Sox vs. the New York Yankees (what is it with Boston?), Burger King vs. McDonald's, and Pepsi vs. Coke.

But, for a time, one of the biggest rivalries in music was between two record companies, one named Motown and the other named Stax.

These two companies were worthy adversaries who had two completely different approaches to music, even down to differences in the sound of their records. And their differences were most profound when it came to demographics.

Motown trademarked the phrase, "The Music of Young America." And that in itself shows the direction of their music and marketing plan. Motown wanted music that was "cross-over" worthy. They wanted to expand the horizons of the black music culture by making music that was at once enjoyed by black America but would also be accepted by young white America. That was their thrust. And history has proven time and again that this plan worked. We all know and love the zillions of great Motown songs.

But during a time of tremendous racial upheaval, Stax Records hit the scene, and their music targeted the African American market. If a song from Stax just happened to cross-over to white America, great. If the song did not, no biggie because young white America was not their demographic.

While Motown had a sign on their building that said, "Hitsville U.S.A." Stax had a sign on their building that said, "Soulsville U.S.A."

When it came to the match-up between Motown and Stax, Motown was serving slices of all-American apple pie, while Stax served slices of down-home Mississippi sweet potato pie.

"The Motown Sound" was smooth and sophisticated. Stax music was raw, earthy, sensual, powerful, and emotionally engaging. We were lucky. We could have a slice of either pie or have them both. My friends, musically speaking, those days were magic.

Stax eventually lost this match-up. Not because they did not have the acts or songs or dedicated management. But in business, as in most things, the devil is in the detail.

A distribution agreement that Stax signed with Atlantic Records contained clauses that gave Atlantic complete ownership of all the Stax master recordings that it was distributing. When, after the fact, Stax discovered this, they were horrified. They had a gold mine, but they had inadvertently given away all the gold inside it. And what good is it to own a gold mine when you do not get to keep the gold?

That one incident began a downward spiral from which Stax was never able to recover.

Today, there is no Stax records, and there has not been for decades, but what a mind-boggling legacy of music and artists it left for us to enjoy.

Here are just a few of the phenomenal acts and artists that recorded on Stax, and I am sure you will remember many of their songs.

Johnnie Taylor gave Stax Records the first platinum record in recording history with his song "Disco Lady." But the song that put Johnnie on the map for me, and I am sure for many of you, was the one that is featured today, called "Who's Making Love."

Jean Knight's tune, "Mr. Big Stuff," was almost like a novelty song to me, and it made me smile every time I heard it. There was just something about the attitude of the song and the way she delivered it.

Sam & Dave had many hit songs on Stax, but "Soul Man" is their signature tune. It is perhaps the only song I have ever heard that created a new name and genre in music.

After "Soul Man" was released and did so well, official music magazines like *Billboard* and *Cashbox* and *Rolling Stone* started referring to and categorizing this style of music as "Soul Music." Soul Music is now called Soul Music because of the worldwide and cultural impact of Sam & Dave's song, "Soul Man." Soul music became the label for the kind of music produced by Stax Records, not Motown.

The Staple Singers were another extraordinary act on the Stax label. And what a unique group line-up. It even included the patriarch of the Staples family, referred to as "Pops" Staples. And one of Pop's daughters, Mavis Staples, was laying down some of the most soulful vocals the world had ever heard, and she did it so effortlessly that it was incredible. Mavis brought "church" right up on stage with her, no matter where she was performing. "Respect Yourself" is another classic song recorded at Stax Records.

The Dramatics did a lot for Stax, beginning with their hit song, "What You See Is What You Get." Ron Banks, the falsetto-singing founder of the group, became a friend. Ron was a great guy. He was kind, funny, super-talented, and not at all pretentious, which he could have been because the Dramatics were flying high. I enjoyed hanging out with Ron as he spent a lot of time in the offices of Wayne Henderson's At Home Productions, where I spent a lot of time writing music.

I think Ron desired to have Wayne—one of the most sought-after producers of his day—produce a solo project with him, though he planned on remaining a member of the Dramatics. I enjoyed listening to Ron as he played his proposed music tracks and sang the lyrics live for Wayne and me to hear.

I was greatly saddened when Ron died. He was only 58 years old. Life on the road can be tough.

Mel & Tim were cousins, discovered by the iconic Gene "The Duke of Earl" Chandler, and Gene produced their first big hit, "Backfield in Motion" on Bamboo Records. Mel & Tim later signed with Stax and recorded the song, "Starting All Over Again."

Albert King (no relation to B.B. King) is one of the greatest bluesmen that ever sang and played the guitar. The name of his massive hit with Stax is "Born Under A Bad Sign," now a blues classic. I think you will enjoy this video, as it has Albert and the great Stevie Ray Vaughn performing this iconic song together. Simply beautiful. Any guitar players out there will especially appreciate this one, as will you blues lovers.

Please remember, this is only a partial list of artists that have recorded hits at Stax records.

There were many more, and some of them have been featured here on *The Saturday Morning Song Chronicles* in the past, like Carla Thomas, Booker T. and the M.G.'s, Otis Redding, and Isaac Hayes. Still, there were others like Eddie Floyd with his song "Knock On Wood," and Fredrick Knight with "Bet You Didn't Know That."

Motown vs. Stax? Not really. Apples and oranges. Each company has immeasurably enriched our lives with their unique approach to music.

Enjoy these rare videos and thank you for taking time out of your busy life to read this book. It has been my great honor to share *The Saturday Morning Song Chronicles* with you.

***

Referenced Videos:

"Who's Making Love"
Johnnie Taylor
https://bit.ly/3cySTYK

"Knock on Wood"
Eddie Floyd
https://bit.ly/2Y47TZc

"Mr. Big Stuff"
Jean Knight
https://bit.ly/2Ms5guZ

"Soul Man"
Sam & Dave
https://bit.ly/2MvvsVr

"Try A Little

Tenderness"
Otis Redding
https://bit.ly/2MpYBS9

"What You See
Is What You Get"
The Dramatics
https://bit.ly/2Y3WJ6M

"Respect Yourself"
The Staple Singers
https://bit.ly/2XuP56k

"Starting All
Over Again"
Mel And Tim
https://bit.ly/3eNLPZF

"Born Under a
Bad Sign."
Albert King
https://bit.ly/32W4S1h

Acknowledgments

To you, my family, friends, and thousands of fans around the world who have enjoyed *The Saturday Morning Song Chronicles* as a column over the past year, I thank you for your love and support.

I would be remiss if I did not issue a special thanks to four of you who inspired me each week, by encouraging me to take *The Saturday Morning Song Chronicles* to the next level. Thank you, Larissa Larissa. Thank you, Joey Joann. Thank you, Sue Melton, and thank you, my brother, Curtis Clay. This book has come into existence because of your suggestions, your love, and your powers of persuasion.

Where things go from here, nobody knows. But *The Saturday Morning Song Chronicles* now enjoys a new life—with endless possibilities—because of the four of you. I am eternally grateful to you all.

My heartfelt thanks to Alice Pasqual for the gorgeous front cover photo. Alice, your work is extraordinary.

Here is Alice Pasqual's link: https://bit.ly/2B9S5fD

About the Author

Paul B Allen III has been a professional in the music industry for nearly fifty years. He has written songs that became *Billboard* magazine number one hits for U.K. Jazz Fusion band Incognito, and for Brothers in Rhythm (on the American charts). His song, "Such A Good Feeling" has been listed as one of the "Greatest 100 Dance Singles of all Time," by the venerable dance music magazine, *Mixmag*.

Allen has also served as the lead vocalist of a legendary vocal group, the Platters ("Only You," "Smoke Gets in Your Eyes," "The Great Pretender"). As such, he has led the group in performances at prestigious venues all around the world, including The Kennedy Center, where the National Symphony Orchestra backed the group. He has also performed for the Royal Family in England, and Prince Albert of Monaco, as well as for the President and First Lady of Fiji.

Allen's style of writing is eclectic. To date, he has completed six books, including The Saturday Mornings Song Chronicles. They are:

Urban Haiku, a hybrid of contemporary urban American haiku housed in traditional Japanese poetic structure.

The Tall Tales of Erasmus Obadiah Short, consisting of whimsical short stories told by "the oldest man in the history of the world."

The Power of X, an anti-superhero science fiction screenplay with a female lead. The story takes place on Earth 2.

Benjamin Franklin: Time Tripper, is a historical science fiction fantasy that began in the colonies before the United States of America and ends up in the Haight Ashbury district of San Francisco in the 1960s.

From Karaoke to The Platters, which contains musical memoirs and a practical step by step guide to breaking into the music industry.

Please enjoy this sample chapter of *From Karaoke to The Platters*

CHAPTER ONE:

LEFT BEHIND

Seventeen words.

Doesn't seem like a lot, does it? But his next seventeen words would change the course of my life forever.

"We're starting a new class in vocal chorus," he began, "and I'll take anyone who can carry a tune."

Wow, we thought, *this is fantastic!*

After all, this was a poor, rural, black school, and this would be the first extra-curricular activity in the school's history. A teacher from a neighboring white school would come here once a week, and we would be excused from the regular reading, writing, and arithmetic, and allowed to do something fun. Sing!

The music teacher listened as each of us, one by one, sang the musical scale he had given. At the end of that marathon session, he would let our fifth-grade teacher know whom to send to the cafeteria for the class that would officially begin the next week.

When the fateful day arrived, 33 of the 35 kids in the class were sent to the cafeteria. Only two hopeless cases were left behind. Their names were Henry and Paul.

As the kids filed out of the classroom, some pointed, while others snickered, at the two "rejects" being left behind.

Though neither Henry nor Paul, appeared to care all that much, inside, Paul was embarrassed and ashamed. I know. I'm Paul.

I have often thought of that music teacher over the decades. Although I never got to attend even one of his classes, each time I think of him, I smile.

As I sang for the Royal Family in England, I thought of him and smiled.

I also thought of him as I sang for Prince Albert of Monaco, and, again, a few days later, when I was invited to the White House to perform for the President of the United States of America.

When I stood before my first audience as the new lead vocalist of The Platters, man, did I smile!

It was an amazing journey, going from "reject" to lead singer of one of the greatest vocal groups of all time. I'd like to tell you the things I did to get from there to here.

Part One, "How I Did It – How You Can Too!" uses autobiographical excerpts from my life to demonstrate the ten steps that changed my world, and that can change yours too, if you're willing to give them a try. Yes, it's true. Just like I did, you can go from singing karaoke to singing on stage as a professional vocalist.

Want to learn how to sing on key? Would you like to improve the quality of your voice?

How about writing music for your own lyrics and poems? Or, would you like to learn how to take any song and put it in YOUR key, making it very easy for you to sing?

Part One gives you all that and more.

Part Two will show you what it's like to be on the road with a world-famous group. You'll see the good, the bad, and the ugly, because if you think it's all fun and games, you are in for a shock.

But also, in Part Two, is a section called "The Perks," which tells you about the upside of being a professional vocalist. You'll learn about the immediate desirability you will gain in the eyes of the opposite sex. You'll learn about the opportunity you have to travel the world in first-class luxury, while getting paid for it, and about the opportunities you will have to meet and work with some of your all-time favorite musical artists, TV personalities, movie stars, and some of the world's most powerful political figures.

Last, but certainly not least, you will learn about the kind of money you can make at this level. You will be amazed.

"The Perks," will convince you that going from karaoke singer to a professional vocalist in a performing group like The Platters is definitely worth the effort!

The trail has been blazed, and you now hold in your hands the only "road map" ever created to help karaoke singers reach their goal of becoming professional vocalists.

This autobiographical map will get you to your desired destination and will show you how to join me in this small, rare, and incredible world I now have the privilege of working in.

The bottom line is this. I'll show you how to go from being a karaoke singer to a professional vocalist, but, in order to balance the scales, I also have to make you aware of *everything* else that will come with the fruition of your musical dreams.

Most of it is fantastic, some of it is terrible, and nearly all of it is unbelievable.

If you're still game, grab your "road map" and take this trip with me now.

You'll find that I'm nothing like that music teacher from my old elementary school. I promise you here and now, I will never leave you behind.

Available at major distributors worldwide.

.

Made in the USA
Monee, IL
10 April 2021